My Parents, My Children

My Parents, My Children

Spiritual Help for Caregivers

CECIL MURPHEY

Westminster John Knox Press
Louisville, Kentucky

Scripture quotations, unless otherwise indicated, are from
the New Revised Standard Version of the Bible, copyright
© 1989 by the Division of Christian Education of the
National Council of the Churches of Christ in the U.S.A.
and are used by permission. Verses marked (NLT) are taken
from *The New Living Translation* © 1996. Used by
permission of Tyndale House Publishers, Inc.,
Wheaton, IL 60189. All rights reserved.

Book design by Sharon Adams
Cover design by Lisa Buckley
Cover photograph: © Ken Redding/CORBIS

First edition
Published by Westminster John Knox Press
Louisville, Kentucky

This book is printed on acid-free paper that meets the American
National Standards Institute Z39.48 standard. ∞

PRINTED IN THE UNITED STATES OF AMERICA

00 01 02 03 04 05 06 07 08 09 — 10 9 8 7 6 5 4 3 2 1

Library of Congress Cataloging-in-Publication Data

Murphey, Cecil B.
  My parents, my children: spiritual help for caregivers/Cecil
    Murphey.—1st ed. p. cm.
  ISBN 0-664-22246-3 (alk. paper)
  1. Caregivers—Religious life. 2. Caring—Religious
    aspects—Christianity. I. Title.
BV4910.9 .M87 2000
248.8'4—dc21

00-028968

In memory of Edith Boehmke

CONTENTS

Part Four: Caring and Feeling   139

Part Five: Caring until the End   199

ACKNOWLEDGMENTS

My special thanks to those who generously shared their experiences with me—many in the midst of their own difficult and demanding situations. Especially, I want to thank Carole Fulmer and Laural Latour for their much-valued advice.

Several have allowed me to tell their stories but chose to remain anonymous. I have respected that request by changing names and some facts.

PART ONE

Learning to Care

Choosing to Care

It seemed as if Mrs. McKamie had always taken care of an invalid husband. Their only son, Edwin, two years my junior, brought me to their house to play one time. We had to whisper and walk around noiselessly. We couldn't even yell in the backyard. After that, I never went back.

As a callused teen, I couldn't figure out why Hannah McKamie hadn't put her husband in some kind of hospital. He was a World War II vet; the government had places for people like him. I asked Mom, who was one of Hannah McKamie's best friends. "Why does she put up with it? She can't go anywhere or do anything. She has to be home all the time."

"Because she loves him," my mother said.

Obviously, she said more than that, but those are the only words I remember. I didn't understand, but even at fourteen years of age I sensed it was the right answer.

As I grew older and my understanding of the world increased, I met or heard about many Hannah McKamies. I admired them and marveled at their commitment.

For instance, shortly after Shirley and I married, we joined the Farnsworth Bible Church. George and Edna Severin, two of the most active members in the congregation, had eight children. Their oldest, George Jr., had been severely retarded since birth.

By the time we met the family, George Jr. was in his twenties. Although well over six feet tall, he barely crawled, spent his days in a large playpen, and couldn't talk. Someone had to feed him and change his diapers.

Yet when I visited, the love in both parents' eyes amazed me. I didn't need to ask why they kept their son at home. In the four years we were in the same church, I never heard either of them complain about the work, the mess, or the demands.

Or I think about Bill and Anna. For five years only an empty lot separated Bill Apostolos's house and mine. His wife, Anna, had Alzheimer's disease. Bill had no culinary skills, so each morning he took their older-model Chevy station wagon out of the garage. They went out for breakfast. They also went out again for lunch.

Bill, in his eighties, didn't speak much about what went on inside the house. Most of us in the neighborhood knew he wasn't a man who allowed others into his private life. In 1998, Bill and Anna moved to live with their older son. I waved as Bill drove that gray Chevy wagon out of our cul-de-sac for the last time. His wife sat on the passenger side, seemingly unaware of their overfilled back seat.

I cite only three situations, but I could give many more. So could most of us. These are examples of people who choose to give long-term care for loved ones. They sometimes put their own lives on hold because they have a greater task.

All around us, people provide long-term care for others. If we examine the situations objectively and without emotion, it does seem strange. Many caregivers become virtual prisoners in their own homes. They regulate their lives by someone else's time clock for medicine, bed change, doctors' appointments, or food. Their social lives—if they have any—hover around getting a friend to come in for a few hours so they can leave.

Why do they do it? Why don't they put people like Anna Apostolos and George Jr. in nursing facilities or institutions? Why do the parents or spouses wear themselves out? Why would they surrender their lives to be unpaid and often-unappreciated maids?

The questions sound cynical and hard, but I asked them in order to make a point.

The answer seems simple enough. Although there are exceptions, most of the caregivers I talked with told me they chose to keep their loved ones at home. Or even if they did put their loved ones in a skilled nursing facility, they were still there to care and to be part of those lives.

Words like *love, responsibility,* and *commitment* flowed from their lips. They said things such as, "I've learned so much about compassion and caring." "His illness has given me meaning and purpose in life."

For instance, after her husband's multiple sclerosis had kept him bedridden for almost three years, Vera Wyman spoke of her previously sheltered, self-centered life. "When Ronnie got sick and couldn't take care of himself, that's when I came alive. Very, very slowly, I saw the world as bigger than me and my needs."

Although I've lost touch with Vera, the last time I saw her she was volunteering at Eggleston Children's Hospital in Atlanta. For Vera, it was a chance to "pay back to God" (her words) for giving her a purpose for being on this planet.

Those who live across the street or on the other side of town admire the caregivers. A few of them are good at saying, "You're a wonderful role model to me for the way you handle all this."

Those are inspiring stories. Some aren't so inspiring, at least not up close. If people would move in for a close-up, they could also see pain, guilt, loneliness, and rejection.

What few outsiders grasp is the daily grind, the ongoing, seemingly endless routines, the problems, frustrations, and confinement of being a caregiver. Most caregivers don't want out, although they have moments when they silently cry for deliverance from their tasks. Some refer to their way of life as a calling. Terry Mobley called it a "divine privilege" to care for her daughter, whose heart defect took the child at age nine.

Some days caregivers' spirits feel drained and their energy lags. They want to scream (and may even do it!).

And yet they persevere.

They hurt inside and often find no arms to engulf them. No quiet voice whispers, "It's all right."

And yet they persevere.

They have doubts about their competence, their purpose, and their intentions.

And yet they persevere.

They feel cut off from the rest of the world and unappreciated.

And yet they persevere.

They have refused to listen to easy answers about "putting him somewhere." They endure the financial hardships, the lack of social companionship. On bad days they long for freedom—just to come and go from the house at will.

Sometimes they cry, and there is no one to hear. God is there, of course, but they also have experiences when heaven's doors seem bolted against them.

Yet they persevere.

They do it because they have chosen to care.

That choice has made the difference. It becomes their badge of courage and the strength that takes them over the bad times.

They are the people who, as my friend Tracy Burkhart says, "Do the next right thing and then the next right thing."

"Do not fear, for I have redeemed you; I have called you by name, you are mine. When you pass through the waters, I will be with you; and through the rivers, they shall not overwhelm you; when you walk through fire you shall not be burned, and the flame shall not consume you. For I am the LORD your God, the Holy One of Israel, your Savior" (Isaiah 43:1b–3a).

Caring God, I have chosen to care. Give me the strength today to fulfill that commitment. Amen.

Making the Choice

Looking back, we did have a choice. Shirley and I could have said no.

Yet for us, it never entered the conscious area of decision making; we simply did it. We took in Edith for one reason—it was the right thing to do.

Edith, an elderly relative, had lost her only son to cancer when he was seventeen. By age 75, she had been a widow for five years after a decade of giving her husband around-the-clock nursing care at home.

Now Edith needed help. Shirley was her closest living relative. Neither of us hesitated. We believed that caring for Edith was our God-given responsibility; we wanted to be faithful to that task.

But yes, we realize now that it was a choice—a long-term choice. Because we believed we were doing the right thing, we made adjustments. Shirley began to work part-time; we bought a house with a mother-in-law suite in the basement so that Edith could live independently with us. In mid-May she moved into her little apartment and seemed to be in relatively good health.

By the end of June, however, medical tests told Edith that her persistent cough was a symptom of congestive heart failure. Six weeks after that she suffered a minor stroke. A woman with great determination, Edith would not give up. She pushed herself to get better. Almost daily she walked through the neighborhood. Or Shirley drove her to a neighborhood park so she could enjoy a quiet view of nature as she walked for half an hour.

Four years after Edith moved in with us, a friendly dog jumped up on her and knocked her down. At the hospital they diagnosed a broken arm and hip. From then on, Edith's health declined.

She lived with us for six and a half years before her death. During those years, Shirley sometimes cried in frustration and a few times in anger, but never in self-pity. She believed we had done the right thing and that God wanted us to care for Edith. During the last nine months, when we felt we had to place her in a skilled-nursing facility, Shirley visited Edith every day to fix her hair, put on her makeup, and sit with her.

I emphasize this because this fact of inner certainty becomes the foundation for Christian caregiving. To work at its best, those who choose to care need to see God's whispered guidance in the situation. They need to offer that care out of love, compassion, and even out of a sense of responsibility. But foremost, they need to see this as their decision to honor God by holding out help-ing hands.

It helps if caregivers can see this as a ministry—a divinely given opportunity to help those in need. We liked to think of it as our giving back to people, like our parents, who loved and cared for us in our early years.

That isn't the way everyone reacts. Too often I have witnessed the elderly being taken in by people who resent the responsibility. They accept the infirm as a bur-den—and it becomes a burden that never goes away.

For instance, my friend Caroline is one of five chil-dren. Her seventy-five-year-old, never-pleased and ever-demanding mother's heart condition and diabetes wouldn't allow her to live alone. That meant someone had to accept responsibility for her.

Caroline's husband refused to have the woman stay in the house for more than a week at a time. "I see what she does to you and how tense you are all the time," he told Caroline. "Your health is more important to me than tak-ing care of her."

After the siblings discussed it at length, one son paid for the mother to travel from Miami to his home in Maui. After six months, he told the others, "I can't keep her anymore."

For the next sixteen months, the siblings grumbled behind the mother's back as they shifted her from family to family. One daughter in Georgia finally agreed to take the mother in. "We need the money," she said. "If she'll turn over her retirement checks, she can live with us."

For two years they kept the woman—and resented every day of it. They bought a new truck and paid for extensive repairs on their home—all from the mother's pension. Yet they constantly grumbled about being forced to keep her.

Caroline's mother is now in a nursing facility, and all the funds are going to pay for her care. "At least now we don't have to fight over who has to take care of her," Caroline said.

When I heard that remark, it saddened me. I've met the mother. Her words sound harsh and impatient, and she expects instant service. But she *is* their mother, I kept thinking. However, it's not for me to criticize them. If I had to live in such a situation, I might understand better. This much, however, I do know. They reluctantly and perhaps angrily accepted a long-term burden.

We chose to care for Edith. Shirley and I never regretted our decision. It was the "next right thing" for us to do.

"Religion that is pure and undefiled before God, the Father, is this: to care for orphans and widows in their distress, and to keep oneself unstained by the world" (James 1:27).

God of the orphans, the fatherless, and the outcasts, help me to make the right choice. Help me to open my heart, do the right thing, and care for those who need me. Amen.

"But I Owe Her"

"But I—I have to. I owe her!"

When Marie said those words, it was the first time I'd heard anyone speak of a debt or obligation to care for a loved one.

"I owe her so much. She sacrificed her life to take care of my two brothers and me."

Other caregivers apparently feel a similar obligation because parents make it evident all through life that it's the expected thing to do when they become old. Most caregivers I've talked with who felt obligated, however, said they took it on themselves, often not discussing it with the aging parent they cared for.

One woman, shocked that I didn't "get it," pulled out her Bible and read from the Ten Commandments: "Honor your father and your mother, so that your days may be long in the land that the LORD your God is giving you" (Exodus 20:12).

"See! Right there it is. You honor them. That means you take care of them because you owe them."

To honor our parents is right, and Paul repeats that command in the New Testament. But how do we do that? Doesn't honor have to do more with respect than it does with becoming slaves—willing or unwilling?

Most of us realize that despite the jarring effects of change in the world, parents and children still need each other. Parents grow old, and they often require assistance from their offspring. When the children care for them, of course, they honor their parents. But does that mean the children *owe* that kind of care? I don't think so.

A few days after I spoke to Marie about owing, I decided to get the perspective of older adults. At a senior citizens function, I asked several people, "What do your children owe you?"

Respect. Love. Those were the two most common responses. When pressed, I heard comments such as, "I'd like to know that my children care."

It amazed me that many of them said, "We don't want to be a burden on them." In two instances, the women began a litany of what they had gone through in caring for their own parents or even grandparents. In effect, both of them said, "I don't want my children to feel the burden of taking care of me the way I felt forced to take care of my mother."

"Don't you want your children to take you in if you need to live with someone?" I asked. They admitted they did, but they also spoke of independence as long as possible, for not wanting their children to feel they *had to* take them in.

"In other words, you don't want them to feel as if they owe you anything?" I asked.

Overwhelmingly they agreed. That may be true, at least ideally. Yet when older adults are in the situation where they need care that they can't give themselves, they naturally look to their children. "Do you feel she owes you a home and the care she provides?" I asked Dora, who had been living with her daughter for nearly four years.

"I hope she doesn't feel that way," she said. "She asked me to live with her. I wouldn't have wanted her to do it under a sense of obligation."

Yet there are those, like Marie, who do feel indebted. For people like Marie, who live under the burden of obligation to a parent, it usually entails anger and resentment—even if well hidden. No one wants to feel like an indentured servant. How much better it is for caregivers, if they take in an aging parent even when they are greatly inconvenienced, to do so because they respect and care for that parent.

Although some parents selfishly demand care, their children will do well to remind themselves, "I choose to help, but I don't *owe* him."

"If I owe you, then it's a contract you signed without consulting me," one son told his demanding father. "I'll help you all I can, but it will be because I want to do it, not because I have to."

The caregivers who can move beyond a sense of indebtedness to helping from compassion and love move in the right direction. The best arrangements occur when the children want to take on the responsibility. "I love him, and he needs me," says it well. The relationship won't be perfect; it wasn't when the caregivers were children at home. It can be a time of mutuality, a time of healing old wounds and fostering healthier relationships.

"Owe no one anything, except to love one another; for the one who loves another has fulfilled the law" (Romans 13:8).

Loving God, help me understand my responsibilities to my loved ones and perform them willingly, not from a sense of obligation. Amen.

The "Why" Question

At some point, most long-term caregivers ask the why question. It's either "Why me, God?" or "Why her?"

Isobel is typical. It took a long time before she realized her mother was suffering from a form of dementia similar to Alzheimer's disease. Once doctors named it, her question became, "Why my mother?" She cried and wept over the painful situation. Her mother had suffered so much that it just didn't seem fair.

Eventually, it became obvious that her mother could no longer live alone. Isobel and Paul took care of her for the next four and a half years. Isobel's mother became increasingly difficult to care for. Although she was demanding and manipulative, there was no question of not keeping her or of putting her in a nursing facility.

During that time, Isobel often asked, "Why me, God?"

Isobel isn't alone. At some point in the midst of their pain and deep agony, most long-term caregivers ask, "Why, God? Why?"

Not only is this a common question among caregivers; it asks more than it implies on the surface.

As a former pastor, I realized long ago that *Why?* may not be the real question.

The worst response I ever heard came from a man at a funeral home. A thirty-nine-year-old mother had died. Her husband couldn't stop weeping. I was there when he asked, "Why? Why did it have to be her? Why couldn't it have been me?"

The husband's friend resorted to reason and explained that life isn't always fair, and that sometimes good people have to suffer as much or more than the wicked. He droned on and even talked about his slain buddies in the Vietnam War.

The bereaved man stopped crying, but I don't think it was because of any of his friend's answers. The lecture—and it really was one—made him feel stupid and selfish for wanting his wife.

Why? may need to be asked—and even encouraged—but it doesn't have to be answered. Even if we had an answer, would it make a difference? Even if God whispered the reason behind the illness, would it change anything? Probably not.

The long-term caregiver still has the burden. The parent is ill, and the child is still caring.

If *Why?* isn't the real question we need answered, what are we really seeking? For each person, the pain behind the question may be quite different.

For one, the inner voice may be pleading, "God, assure me that you're with me. Help me know you care." To another, the question may be prompted by fears of inadequacy to cope.

Some find the question difficult to ask, as if they are demanding God to become accountable. Others are ashamed for being weak enough to ask.

I've learned one thing from this question. It's wonderfully freeing to ask. Those who have wept and asked repeatedly have told me that they often found relief—perhaps not peace, but some rest from the turmoil—by simply asking the question aloud and allowing their hearts to speak the anguish they feel.

"I wasn't questioning God as much as I was trying to make sense out of life," Etta Jordan told me. "My husband of forty years had been the strong one and had done everything for the children and me. Then he became an invalid, and it didn't make sense to me."

Maybe that's where we have to start. We need to make sense of the situation. "If I'd thought about it, I would have realized that one day we'd have to take care of one of my parents," Isobel said later. "Paul and I had our lives planned out. As soon as our third child left the nest, we'd both be in our late forties, and we would travel and enjoy the things we couldn't afford to do." Her mother's illness canceled their plans. "We didn't even have a real vacation during those years. Mom made everyone else so miserable! Three days was the maximum anyone could stand her."

Isobel made room for her mother, but the question kept erupting: "Why? Why us? It just didn't make sense. It shouldn't have happened to us," she kept saying.

Did Isobel ever answer her own question? Not really. Instead, she learned to shift her focus. Slowly she realized there was nothing she could do to change the situation. "Help me accept what I have to accept."

As one source of peace, she prayed the well-known Serenity Prayer adopted by Alcoholics Anonymous: "God, grant me the serenity to accept the things I cannot change, the courage to change the things I can, and the wisdom to know the difference" (attributed to Reinhold Niebuhr).

For Isobel, acceptance was what she sought and found.

Acceptance. That's where many struggle. As long as they keep saying, "Life isn't supposed to work like this," they're stuck in their confusion and pain. Once they can say, "This is the way life is," they no longer need to answer the question.

Isobel got beyond the question by what we sometimes call reframing. She began to think of the benefits and the blessings instead of the struggles and the demands. That wasn't an easy task. She grew in her commitment to God and in her relationship with her husband, but she also learned valuable lessons.

"I was a selfish person," Isobel said. "I never thought much about people who were in such situations. I promised God that once I got through this, I would reach out and help others." Although she prefers not to have her real name known, she has made it her ministry in her church and community to visit and encourage caregivers.

"I know that God is with me," she said. "Nothing will ever separate me from that love."

"For I am convinced that neither death, nor life, nor angels, nor rulers, nor things present, nor things to come, nor powers, nor height, nor depth, nor anything else in all creation, will be able to separate us from the love of God in Christ Jesus our Lord" (Romans 8:38–39).

Understanding God, remind me that it's all right to ask questions that have no valid answers. Help me understand that I don't always need answers. It is even more important for me to accept what I cannot change—and I rely on your help. Amen.

Power Reversal

"When I was a little girl, Mama brushed my long, blonde hair, and I loved the feel of the flannel cloth when she gently washed my face," Earline said. "We often talked about which dress I was to wear that day. Most of the time, she let me choose."

Earline stared into space for a long time. "Now it's gone the other way, hasn't it? In some ways, it's like taking care of my own child. It's sad, really sad, that our lives have reversed."

Roles do change. It's not easy for everyone to grasp that fact, especially not an aging parent. Older children don't need their parents as they did when they were younger. They learn to make their own decisions and to live independently. Then illness forces changes, and the older generation needs the younger's help. For some parents, that's a frightening experience. Unsure of their children's love or commitment, they may become manipulative or demanding. Or they may withdraw.

It's difficult for a father to become the "child" of his own offspring. It speaks of dependency and loss of freedom. It means giving up the final reality of adulthood.

"I'm your mother, that's why. You do as I say."

"You listen to me. I've lived a lot longer than you have, and I know a few things."

Like most children, Earline had grown up hearing those remarks. Now they're no longer appropriate. Her mother has to relinquish authority. The two must switch power roles. How do they do it?

"I was asking Mama to do what I told her," Earline said. "It's difficult for a woman of seventy-five to surrender control to her forty-seven-year-old daughter.

"The worst part of having my mother live with us

wasn't the caregiving itself. That was the easy part—or maybe I was prepared for that. But to have her nag me for not turning off a light or forgetting to close the closet door—in my own house—was the worst part. She'd use that tone of voice I remember as a kid: 'Now wipe your feet.' 'Don't come to the table with those dirty hands.' "

If a parent is sick enough or compliant enough, this may not present a problem. However, when a person has held the reins of power, has made the major decisions, has guided and been relied on for strength in difficult times, it's not easy to let go.

"We had a big battle the first day," Earline said. "Mama wasn't being mean or difficult. She was just being the mother she had always been. Right then, I realized things had to change or life would be a nightmare for me."

"What did you do?" I asked, because I knew her mother was still alive, lived with her, and they got along well.

"I looked right into those deep brown eyes and said, 'Mama, you gotta move on if you're gonna move in. You can't tell me what to do or make all the decisions. I'm in charge now.' "

Earline laughed. "Sounds cold, but I knew I had to say those words to her. She didn't realize how bossy she was." The words didn't sink in right away, but they set the tone for their new relationship.

Part of the role reversal is for the caregiver to understand and to accept a parent's aging. In some ways, the parent is no longer the person he or she once was.

It reminds me of the final scene of the film version of "Driving Miss Daisy." Hoke, her former chauffeur, visits Daisy in a nursing facility and feeds her pumpkin pie. She smiles and says, "Hoke, you're my best friend."

This was a poignant moment, but rather sad. The vibrant, strong-willed, feisty Miss Daisy had become dependent, like a young child. She had to rely on others to help her eat her food.

This happened in our caring for Edith. After her stroke and heart attack, dementia set in. Sometimes she would behave childishly. She'd talk, and if someone tried to speak, she'd raise her voice and get louder.

One day, she went on for a long time about something that had happened to her son when he was five—a story we had heard many times. Without pausing, she began to repeat it.

Shirley took her hand, and said firmly, "All right, Edith, be quiet."

Looking back, I think it was one of the hardest things Shirley ever had to do, but it was the right thing. It sounded like a mother speaking to her daughter.

Edith stopped talking.

In that moment, I believe all three of us knew the balance of power had shifted. Edith was in our care, and we were setting the rules.

To her credit, Edith never argued. Many times she thanked us for taking her in and for caring for her. When she spoke with others, she told them how good we were to her. She accepted the power reversal.

Not everyone does.

The power shifts whether the awareness happens over a period of weeks or in a moment—as it did with Edith. What matters is that, as the person becomes sicker, the caregiver has to assume more responsibility.

Just to realize what's happening enables many to cope better.

Earline faced a common problem of many adult children. She needed to figure how to reverse the power role—and it is a power role—and help her mother maintain dignity. "I wanted us to be two adults. Someone had to be in charge and make decisions."

When I asked others how they coped, of the variety of responses here are three that seemed the most helpful in the sometimes ongoing power reversal.

"You have the right to say that, but I don't have to agree."

"Yes, I know your needs are as important as mine, and mine are not less important than yours."

"You used to say that as long as I lived in your house, I had to obey your rules. And I did. Now you're living in my house, and we go by *my* rules."

Earline tried to make it easier for her mother. She ignored the parental demands. She became adept at asking questions that gave choices. "Would you like your bath now, Mama, or do you want to wait a little?" She asked her mother to choose the clothes she would wear that day. "If I gave her choices, it was a way of talking to an adult. She had given up enough personal control of her life; I didn't want to take away her dignity as well."

As we become aware of the shifting of roles, power, and responsibility, we may need to remind ourselves, "She is a human being. She is my mother and not my child."

[Jesus' words to Peter] "Very truly, I tell you, when you were younger, you used to fasten your own belt and to go wherever you wished. But when you grow old, you will stretch out your hands, and someone else will fasten a belt around you and take you where you do not wish to go" (John 21:18).

All-powerful God, at times it feels as if I'm caring for a child, but I'm not. Remind me that this is a person who deserves my respect. Help me to do whatever I can to preserve his/her dignity. Amen.

Growing Up

"I thought I had finally grown up," Judith Raines said. "I don't remember ever liking my father very much. He and my mother divorced when I was nine, and I never lived with him again. He came around occasionally to take my brother and me to a baseball game or a movie, but that's about all."

She spoke of his bad temper and how quickly his words became abusive to anyone who disagreed with him. He called regularly and tried to tell her how to run her life, and he kept laying down rules for her behavior. "I pay for your support, so I can do that!" he yelled once.

After she married, she heard from him less often. But when she did, he was the advice machine, always telling her how to run her life. Many times she slammed the phone down in anger.

"When I was thirty-one, I felt I had finally grown up, because that's when I decided to cut Dad out of my life." To make that clear to him, she went to visit, told him how much she had disliked him, and walked out the door as soon as she said, "I never want to see you again."

She had grown up. Or had she?

What does it mean to grow up? Does it mean we pass through certain stages in life? We're born totally dependent on someone else; we're not mature until we're able to do everything on our own. Then what? Most of us, if we live long enough, end up in a kind of dependency different from what we started with.

Sometimes we call the growing process *separation-individuation*. It's the way we achieve identity. We reach the point of becoming autonomous, which may make us feel like the fabled John Wayne or other invincible heroes in films. We don't need anybody!

But there's more to growing up than that. Maturing implies that we have a sense of separation or individuation. Most of us also know that it can't come at the cost of losing our connection. When we were younger, we had to keep running back to our parents for security. In psychological circles they call that *reapproachment*.

Many fail to realize that reapproachment doesn't end when children reach a certain age, leave home, or voluntarily cut off contact. Whether we want to face it or not, that unexplainable, perhaps mystical connection is always there—part of the way God created human beings. I doubt that any of us fully gives up the need and the desire for parental approval—and that approval doesn't matter whether the parents are alive or dead.

Ultramarathon runner Stan Cottrell has often made this clear to me. He's in his fifties, and his father's been dead more than twenty years. Yet Stan realizes that even now, he's still trying to please his father, somehow—at long last—to gain approval. He'll never hear the words he yearns for.

Judith, however, insisted that she had been emancipated. "For fourteen years I insisted that I was one of the slaves set free. I would never go back into bondage again." She often told her friends of her terrible childhood, and concluded, "And now I'm free."

One insightful friend asked, "If you're so free, why do you talk about your father so much?"

That question shocked Judith. She hadn't realized how often she mentioned him. Slowly she did begin to realize that, like it or not, she was tied to him with invisible cords.

As much as she hated to admit it, her father had become an instrument of comparison. She frequently said things such as, "I'm more giving than my father." "I listen; Dad never did." At other times she'd say, "I have Dad's temper. Sometimes I flare up at people. But I'm different in that I feel bad about it afterward. I doubt that he ever apologized."

That's when Judith admitted to herself that she had never been fully emancipated. All through the years, thoughts of her father intruded. Occasionally, anger toward him would arise. At other times, she'd remember longing to hear a single word of approval. She had been fooling herself. Dad was still a vital part of her life, even though she didn't like it.

Then one day her father phoned from half a continent away. "I'm sick and can't work. I can't live alone much longer." He begged her to let him live with her. He asked forgiveness and made every kind of promise that he wouldn't interfere with her life.

Judith took him in because she felt she had no choice. Even when she said yes, she knew her father wouldn't change—probably couldn't change.

Her father is with her. They have their verbal differences, but they're far less volatile than they were during her childhood. She doesn't know if she and her father will ever have the warmth and harmony that marks happy family relationships.

"I know this. I've grown up." Her eyes twinkled as she said, "And you know what? Growing up doesn't mean getting away from my father. Growing up means connecting with him. Some days I hate him—I really feel that way. Most of the time, I feel sorry for him, and sadness comes over me that it took us so long to get together. Sometimes I think that we could have had a deep, loving relationship if both of us had just tried a little harder."

Judith also knows that growing up means accepting

life as it happens. She has softened toward her father. In his own way, he's made strides. He's even begun to thank her—something he never did before.

Now she lives with hope. "My dream is that before he dies, I can say without reservation that I love him and that I'm thrilled he's my father." She smiles. "I also hope that he'll tell me how important I am in his life. That may never happen, but who knows? Maybe both of us will grow up before it's too late."

"'Honor your father and mother'—this is the first commandment with a promise: 'so that it may be well with you and you may live long on the earth'" (Ephesians 6:2).

God, our all-loving Parent, help me always to know that your deep love and compassion bind me to yourself. Help me also to accept that, as part of your design, I'm bound to my parents. Amen.

All You Can Do

"It's never enough. No matter what I do for her, I go to bed feeling I should have done a lot of other things." When pressed, Tina went through a litany of how she should have anticipated her mother's wants or how she had failed her mother by her insensitivity. "The other day, I just forgot about her medicine. When I remembered, I was nearly an hour late, and she was hurting badly."

Because of two previous conversations, I was aware that no matter how hard Tina tries, she feels she never does enough for her mother.

"All you can do is all you can do," her husband, Phil, says to her from time to time. "When is enough enough?" he asks.

Tina, like a lot of caregivers, cuts corners in life—her own corners. She shortchanges her own happiness to "do right by" her mother. In the past year she has virtually given up her social life. She works outside the home five hours a day, and she has been trying to figure out how the family can get by without the money she brings in so she can be home with her mother.

Others don't make such drastic changes, but they still shortchange themselves by pulling back. Too often they give up the things that relaxed them or gave them pleasure. "I just don't have time for things like that," one woman said when asked to re-join her tennis team.

After Edith's stroke, Shirley stopped playing the organ, something she found relaxing and enjoyable. Even though she knew it was good therapy, she said, "When I do find time to enjoy myself, I don't have any energy left to do it."

Others tell me they gave up hobbies or going to lunch

with their friends, or they dropped membership in organizations. Because of their commitment to care, they curtailed their own lives.

The popular term today is *setting boundaries.* Caregivers need a healthy sense of themselves and of those they care about, and they need to draw distinct lines between the two.

Tina had torn down the separateness and had begun to take on the feelings and responsibilities that belonged to her mother. It was difficult for her to accept that her role was to be *with* her mother and not to take responsibility for her mother's life.

Some caregivers can never do enough. No matter what they do, it still won't be enough.

"You mean your sick mother's life is more important that yours?" asked Phil. "Or more important than our children and me?"

"Not more important, just—well, just more urgent. She needs help; there are so many things she can't do for herself."

"And we can do for ourselves? But what about you? Aren't you entitled to a life?" He wanted to get a point across. He didn't feel neglected, and neither did the children. His wife was his concern. "You have a life, and you have the right to live it too."

He wasn't urging her not to care for her mother. "Do what you can, then stop. Make her an important priority, but not your entire life."

In this instance, all the family members talked with Tina's mother. To their surprise, the mother responded, "You've been wonderful to me. You've already done more than I could have expected."

Those words alleviated much of Tina's confusion and turmoil.

Not everyone has the considerate parent who can do that. Regardless, adult children need to accept limitations. For their own sake and for the sake of other family members, they need to draw boundaries. In doing so, they may need to call on others to help them with their feelings of selfishness and neglect.

"Do not fear, for I am with you, do not be afraid, for I am your God; I will strengthen you, I will help you, I will uphold you with my victorious right hand" (Isaiah 41:10).

All-loving God, help me know when to stop. Give me wisdom and strength to set the right boundaries. Amen.

But She Refused Help!

"She's so stubborn at times!" Shirley said about Edith. The doctor had given Edith a heart medicine, and she refused to take it.

"I'm not going to put that rat poison into my body," she said. "It may help my heart, but it will destroy something else. That's the way medicine works."

It took several days of patiently reasoning with her before Edith finally agreed to take her medication. Even then, for several weeks Shirley had to keep checking on her. "Oh, I've already taken it today," she'd say, even though Shirley knew from the number of remaining pills that she hadn't.

This situation isn't that unusual. We constantly find that those in our care don't want our help. They resent our input. They try to block us out.

Others have told their stories. "He won't listen to what I tell him," one son said of his father's insistence on smoking a cigar every night. I keep telling him it's not good for him, and he knows, but he keeps on anyway."

That's part of the dilemma we face in giving long-term care. We're dealing with human beings. Even if they are incapacitated, it's still their lives. To a point at least they have the right to maintain their own lives.

Where is that point? I think of Naomi, a woman in the church I used to pastor. She went to one doctor for nearly twenty-five years. During the last ten years before he retired, Naomi saw him regularly. When she complained and asked for medication, he gave it to her, often without fully examining her.

Naomi became increasingly dependent on prescription drugs. Several members of her family believed that the doctor gave her more than she needed. They tried to get her to change doctors, but Naomi wouldn't listen.

Her doctor was getting elderly, and Naomi's family suspected he wasn't keeping up with medical advancements. Even after he retired, he continued to treat a few patients in his home. Naomi was one of them.

Her doctor's death forced Naomi to find another doctor. Previously, she had been loquacious and rarely stopped talking. She constantly complained of pains all through her body and seldom left the house. Her new doctor cut her medicine down to a fraction of what she had been getting. For the next three years, the change in her seemed like a miracle. Until she had her first stroke at age seventy-eight, Naomi was a changed woman. She stopped her incessant talking and rarely complained of pain. She went out socially, attended church regularly, and began to volunteer in the nursery.

"Should we have intervened before the doctor's death?" her family asked me. There's no answer to that one, but it is a question many caregivers need to consider.

"What do we do when Dad resists our efforts to help him, to talk about his health or his medication? Even though Mom withholds information, should I pry or push? How much do I assert myself?"

As a general rule, if it's not a serious or life-threatening situation, the person has a right to make choices, even if those choices may be unwise or even foolish.

In talking to a variety of people, most of them suggest that the caregiver present a case and express concern. If the parent still insists on ignoring it, they advise, "Back down. It's out of your hands."

When the problems become serious, caregivers may have to intervene. In those instances, they need to assert themselves and even to take over if necessary.

Here's one hint a caregiver passed on. If the person refuses, say, "Then do this for me." In a few instances, we had to use that with Edith. We knew she was grateful that we had taken her into our home. The one argument that always worked—and we made it one of last resort—was for Shirley to say these words: "If you won't do it for yourself, then do it for me. I'll worry a lot less, and it will make less work for me."

It reaches the point where the caregiver finally has to say, "I know what she needs. I will be remiss in my responsibility if I don't intervene." To push and to insist may make us feel like villains, but when another's health is involved, we do what we do out of that person's need even though it violates their privacy or their sense of propriety. It may help to remind ourselves: We who care have responsibility for our loved ones. Responsibility may mean intervention, even if the loved one resists our help.

"I pray that the God of our Lord Jesus Christ, the Father of glory, may give you a spirit of wisdom and revelation as you come to know him" (Ephesians 1:17).

All-caring God, enable me always to love and to care, and help me know when to intervene and when to back off. Amen.

Being a Nonperson

Years ago, two of us stood talking outside a theater. A man pushed a wheelchair past us. Although we continued our conversation, both of us watched. He stopped next to a dark blue Honda, unlocked the passenger's door, and helped the woman in the wheelchair stand up. Even from twenty feet away, it was obvious that her pain made it difficult for her to move. Once the man helped her inside, he folded the wheelchair, put it in the trunk, got in on his side, and they drove off.

"Poor woman," I said. "She must live in terrible pain."

After the car drove away, my friend said, "I'll bet you could describe the woman in the wheelchair, couldn't you?" After I nodded, he said, "But I'll also bet you don't remember nearly as much about the man, do you?"

"Why, he was—" Then I realized I had hardly noticed him. He was just an older man.

Since then, I've realized that's how many of us view such couples. The caregiver easily becomes a nonperson. The sick one receives the attention and the concern.

"At first, that was fine. I was concerned about Fred too," Betty Arnold said of her husband, diagnosed with congestive heart failure and emphysema. "I watched him closely. Each time I saw an increased loss of control in his body, I fretted. More and more I took over for Fred, doing things he couldn't do for himself."

After a few months, Betty began to wonder why people didn't ask how she was—really ask. They had begun to see her as an extension of Fred. "Or maybe it's my feeling of being invisible more than it's their attitude. When they talk to me, their question is usually, 'How is Fred doing now?' It's as if I'm a nonperson."

As Fred's condition worsened, his needs increased.

33

"That's how it goes," Betty said. "The task doubles and the energy halves." She now does all the outside things Fred did, such as cleaning gutters, cutting the grass, and raking leaves.

"Many days I feel exhausted from all the demands on my time and from watching his limitations grow. I sure wish things were different." Then she paused and smiled. "You know, your coming to talk to me means a lot. You're treating me like I'm a real human being. I need to feel that I'm more than an extension of Fred. I don't want to be so invisible that I'm nobody by myself. Everybody wants to be seen as a person, don't you think?" she asked.

Yes, they do. Betty Arnold is a person. She's a caregiver who is devoted to her husband. But foremost, Betty is a real person.

"Do not fear, for I have redeemed you; I have called you by name, you are mine" (Isaiah 43:1b).

All-knowing God, sometimes I feel totally alone and invisible to everyone, but you know my name, you care. Help me always to remember that. Amen.

Compartmentalizing Life

"Two years ago, if someone had told me to compartmentalize, I would have laughed," Jan Toothman said. "How do you shut off your feelings? Is it like pressing a button?"

Yet Jan learned that her emotional survival depended on doing just that.

Jan's mother had come to live with the family two years earlier. At seventy-three, her physical condition had begun to deteriorate, but she functioned without a lot of assistance. She cooked the evening meal and did some light housework. After recovery from her first stroke, Jan's mother's skills diminished, but she still cooked dinner and set the table.

Although Jan's mother didn't have another stroke, other aggravating conditions surfaced. Her balance became an ongoing problem. Several times a week while Jan was at work, her mother fell. Finally she was in a wheelchair. At the end of two years, her mother went into a skilled nursing facility.

Jan paid a quick visit to her mother every morning on her way to work. She stopped by for an hour after work. The worst part was that she thought about her mother virtually all day long. It disrupted her work, making her less efficient.

"You need to forget your mother when you leave home and not think of her all day long," a co-worker said. "Pick up the concern again when you leave the office."

"At first it made me furious," Jan said. "My co-worker had a great life with no problems. Who was she to tell me what to do?" The more Jan thought about it, the more she admitted that, although not given too tactfully, it was good advice.

"How do I compartmentalize?" she kept asking herself. "How do I stop thinking about Mother throughout the day?"

Jan asked other caregivers, and to her amazement, many of them made no effort to compartmentalize. "Just live with it!" one angry person said.

Although she learned various ways that people used, Jan found one method that worked for her. Whenever she became aware that her mind was on her mother, she snapped her fingers.

"Sounds silly, but it works," she told me. "That simple, physical action is enough for me to shove thoughts about Mother into a back compartment of my mind." She confessed that it took her at least two weeks before that worked effectively.

Snapping the fingers doesn't work for everyone. One woman told me, "I say 'Yes' aloud. Unfortunately, sometimes people stare or ask me what I mean." She usually smiles and says, "Oh, nothing." But it's effective for her.

One of the most interesting compartmentalization techniques (and it sounded the simplest) came from Julie. "Each day I visualize that when I enter the door of our building and close it behind me, I'm closing out that part of my life. When I leave work and open the door, then I visualize starting my home life again." Unless she gets a phone call at work, she has learned to push thoughts of caregiving away.

Some caregivers don't have jobs away from the home. Although they have to live in the situations twenty-four hours a day, they can also learn simple methods.

Time alone. Time to pray, read, walk. Those down times of escape from the situation—times away from the loved one—equip them to return with new energy.

"Finally, beloved, whatever is true, whatever is honorable, whatever is just, whatever is pure, whatever is pleasing, whatever is commendable, if there is any excellence and if there is anything worthy of praise, think about these things . . . and the God of peace will be with you" (Philippians 4:8–9).

Caring God, you do care about me and every part of my life. Help me temporarily to lay aside my burdens when it's the wise thing to do. Amen.

"She's Your Mother"

Dick's mother needed family care, and his wife, Emma, became the primary caregiver.

In such a situation, if both women like each other the arrangement often works well, but Dick's mother didn't particularly like Emma and hadn't treated her kindly—at least that was Emma's perception. Dick was aware of their quiet dislike for each other.

Dick naively assumed that Emma would welcome his mother into their home. Emma didn't object at first. The longer Dick's mother stayed, however, the tenser the relationship became.

Finally, Emma screamed, "I can't stand her. You take care of her. She's *your* mother!" Emma later admitted that she had lost control, but that explosion changed things.

Emma wanted to help. There were things, such as bathing Dick's mother, she was quite willing to do. But she insisted that Dick take on more responsibility. "She doesn't like me and makes no effort to conceal it. *You* listen to her complaints. *You* carry her food to her. *You* take over so that I don't have to spend half my day in there."

To his credit, Dick did help where he could.

But where do we draw the line? Who cares for whom? When it's the husband's mother, does that require less of the wife? Or when it's the wife's parent, does that mean more?

It's a tangled issue, and if it remains on an emotional level, the relationship gets worse. It would have helped if the two women had talked about their differences, or even if Emma had said to her mother-in-law, "I'll help as much as I can, but when Dick comes home from work, he will be the one helping you."

The best approach—whenever possible—is to bury the whose-mother-is-it question. Both Emma and Dick need to say to each other, "We have chosen to care for her. She needs us, and we'll give her the best care we're capable of giving."

That means that Emma and Dick put aside petty differences or slights that occurred twenty years earlier. They may need to confront some of those issues and bring them into the open. But usually, when a person is willing to bathe an older parent and assist in personal grooming, the past dissolves between them.

When I heard the story, I admired Emma's conclusion: "I'm doing this because it's the right thing. I believe God wants me to do it. I still don't like her very much, but I'm doing all I can for her."

[Jesus said] "I was sick and you took care of me" (Matthew 25:36b).

Loving God, remind me that when I serve others, I am serving you. Amen.

Life Lessons

"Maybe I wasn't listening properly in Sunday school," Marcia Mullins said. "I grew up thinking that life was going to work out— if not perfectly, at least pretty good. We had God. Why wouldn't things work out?"

Marcia will quickly tell you that she had a rather uneventful life until she was thirty-seven. She married Dan, her college sweetheart, and they had two children. Dan's sales skills led him upward to a high-paying management job within ten years. "Then our lives fell apart," she said.

Marcia was driving one day with their son Danny, who was ten. Two teens were playing chicken; one of them hit the Mullins's car. It rolled over and down an embankment. Marcia had minor injuries, but Danny's spine was crushed. Marcia quit her job and stayed home to work with her son and worked with him through exercises provided by a physical therapist. Three years later, Danny took his first steps.

While Danny was still unable to walk, Marcia's mother suffered a stroke, leaving her partially paralyzed on her left side. Because Marcia was an only child, her mother moved in with the family.

"My world crashed. It had been bad enough when our son was hurt. I had no idea how I could possibly cope with my mother as well. But I did, you know." Marcia's bright smile affirmed it.

Friends marveled at Marcia's ability to adapt to the demands. A few wondered if she was putting on a false front in public and collapsing at home. But as the days continued, even the most cynical saw that the public Marcia was the true one.

Some days the tiredness showed on her face. Occasionally, she canceled social gatherings. Instead of teaching four-year-olds every Sunday, she set up a team so she would be covered when she couldn't make it.

Most of them marveled that Marcia never complained. "I finally figured out that this really is the way life works," she told a few of us. "I didn't ask for this, and I sure wish it wasn't this way, but this is how it is. So we learn to make the best of it."

Perhaps six months after her mother moved in, Marcia told me her secret, and then laughed because she didn't think it was a secret. "I live by Philippians 4:13 and Romans 8:28. When Dan and I dated, we decided to take those two verses to heart for the rest of our lives. When I start feeling sorry for myself or thinking I can't cope, I quote them. Or I look them up in various translations. They never fail to lift my spirits so that I can cope again.

"These are life's lessons—not the lessons I would choose. This is what God has chosen for me. I told God many years ago that I'd follow wherever the path led. This one has had rough places, but God has made me able to handle it."

Some lessons may be harder than others, and some of us seem to have more than our share of hardship. When we see that this is the way it is and that God can enable us to cope—and give us the strength we need as hardship comes—we learn. We grow. We also enrich others.

"I can do all things through him who strengthens me" (Philippians 4:13).

"We know that all things work together for good for those who love God, who are called according to his purpose" (Romans 8:28).

God of wisdom, love, and power, thank you for strength, for the ability to stand up and handle the worst of situations. Amen.

My Needs?

Wilma Knight's embarrassment showed when we talked about caregivers' needs. "Forget your Dad right now. Tell me about Wilma," I said. "What needs do you have?"

She shrugged. "It's a load at times, but, you know, I'm all right."

"Are you sure?" I persisted.

"Oh, I get down from time to time." Wilma cares for her mother. Her husband travels for a large corporation and is home only on weekends. "We cope. We really do."

As we talked more, she told me about her coping methods. "First, I have a support system. There are seven of us, and we stay in touch daily because we have an elderly parent in our home." Wilma, a member of a large metropolitan church that follows the Stephens Ministry program, set this up long before her mother became ill.

"We call each other by phone. Four of us are on e-mail, and we send little words of encouragement to each other. We've met a couple of times in person, but it's really hard for all of us to get together physically. Mostly, we reach out to each other by phone or e-mail."

Wilma handed me a copy of an e-mail she had received from one of the group members that day:

> Kindness is the language which the deaf can hear and the blind can see.—*Mark Twain.*

Wilma shared another thing she does. On 3 × 5 file cards she has written simple, positive statements. One of them says, "God loves me, and God always cares for me." Another card reads, "With God's help, I can handle anything that happens to me today."

Wilma has perhaps twenty such cards and adds to

them regularly or occasionally throws one away that's no longer meaningful. She reads and repeats each statement several times every day.

"It's my way to pump out the sludge and allow the clean waters to come in." She said that it's easy for her to think negatively as she watches her mother's condition go downhill. "As Mother hurts more, I have to work hard at not feeling bad as well. Daily doses of those cards help."

Long ago she realized that people frequently ask about her mother. Why not? She's sick, and it touches her that they care. "Even if they ask, 'How are you?' I assume they're being polite, and they don't want to know all the details."

Like others I've met, Wilma finds it easier to shut out most people's polite questions and to share her honest answers with those who know and understand her situation.

"Of course, I have needs," she confesses. "So do other caregivers. Because we understand, we can strengthen each other."

"And my God will fully satisfy every need of yours according to his riches in glory in Christ Jesus" (Philippians 4:19).

God of compassion, forgive me for ignoring my needs or for thinking I'm the only one in this situation. Help me receive help, and enable me to reach out to others. Amen.

Pleasing Mom

Lucy's mom was a perfectionist. She would never leave the house until she had made the beds, put away dishes, and at least vacuumed the den. She spent inordinate amounts of time on her hair and appearance. Everything had to look exactly right.

"That was okay for her, but she also expected me to be perfect. Consequently, nothing I did pleased her," Lucy said. "No matter what I did, it wasn't good enough." For example, one day Lucy cleaned her mother's house; she spent most of two days cleaning while her mother was hospitalized. When her mother came home, she looked around, sniffed, and said, "You used that cheap furniture polish, didn't you?"

To make it worse, Lucy's sister is named Linda. Although both have the same initial sounds, Lucy grew up feeling that Linda was the preferred child. It hurt her deeply when her mother called her Linda. "I guess she wishes that I were Linda," she often thought.

All through her life, Lucy has tried to please her mother. Yet she felt that no matter how hard she tried, what she did was never quite perfect; consequently, it was never quite good enough.

Then, unable to keep up her house alone, her mother moved in with Lucy. Within two days, Lucy learned everything she did wrong in her house from her choice of furniture to the way she disciplined her children.

One morning, her mother sat in the kitchen having breakfast. Lucy, already running late, rushed through her morning tasks.

"You know, this color is wrong for this room," her mother said. "It makes the kitchen look small and dark."

Lucy banged her purse on the counter. "Is there

anything you do like around here? Just one thing? Have I ever done anything that pleased you—ever—in my entire life?"

Never had Lucy spoken like that to her mother. "What is wrong with you today?"

"Today? I'm angry. I've been angry a long time. I've spent most of my life trying to please you, and nothing ever does. Do you realize that you never say anything complimentary to me? You have been here four days, and you've spent most of that time telling me what I do wrong *in my own home.*"

"I was merely offering suggestions—"

"No, you were criticizing me, and I can't take any more. We took you in. I hoped that just taking you in would at last be something I did right. But you're still the same critical, harsh mother you've always been!"

Lucy grabbed her purse and ran from the house. She cried all the way to work. But in her tears, she also found some relief. She had spoken up for herself at last. She knew that trying to please Mom would go on, and it would be an ongoing battle, but now she wouldn't have to listen to the criticism.

At dinner her mother said to Lucy's husband, "I've been afraid to open my mouth this evening. Apparently, I offend Lucy whenever I speak."

"Yes, you do," he said, "and I don't like it." He leaned across the table and said, "We invited you into our home because you're Lucy's mother. She loves you even though she has never felt you loved her."

"Of course, I love her! I'm her mother!"

"It's not the same thing," Lucy said.

"But I do! I do love you!"

A year later, the mother is still in the house and becoming more frail. Occasionally she still offers unwanted advice—the kind that hurts her daughter.

"Thank you, but I don't agree." That has become Lucy's stock answer. Surprisingly, it works.

Lucy wishes for a warm relationship with her mother. She's realistic enough to know that probably won't take place. A part of Lucy will go on the rest of her life trying to please Mom. But at least she's more aware of that, and she's standing up for herself.

"As long as I please God, my family, and myself, that's enough." Lucy smiled. "Okay, I'm not really there yet, but that's my goal."

"When the ways of people please the LORD, he causes even their enemies to be at peace with them" (Proverbs 16:7).

Forgiving God, forgive me for the wrong focus in my life. I've tried so hard to please Mom, when I need more to learn to please you. Amen.

Helpful Words?

Edith had been diagnosed with colon cancer. Shirley called our pastor, and someone put Edith on the prayer chain. That's a weekly list that travels by e-mail or phone to those who sign up to pray for each need.

When we went to church the following Sunday, a number of people offered kind and consoling words. Some of them were simple, such as "I'm sorry" or "It must be hard on you."

Others said words that, at best, didn't help. In some cases, they made Shirley feel worse. These people meant well. They searched for the right words to say, such as exhortations or cheerful words that would give her a pickup. They wanted to brighten her day and help her view the situation more positively.

Here are some of the well-meant words that Shirley received. As a caregiver, you've probably heard them all:

–"Now, don't cry. You'll just make yourself sick."
–"Hey, I know it's sad, but it's not the end of the world. You'll get past this."
–"One day you'll look back and be stronger and more mature because of this experience."
–"Just hang in there. It will get better."
–"Oh, I know exactly how you feel."
–"Just be positive." (Or "Be strong" or "Be brave." Anything that tells you what to "be.")

None of these helped, despite the solicitation or good intentions of the speaker.

So what do we say or do when people offer these clichés? The simple, easiest thing is to say "Thank you" and go on.

Some experts advise caregivers to challenge rather

than fret afterward. If you do challenge, make it as tactful and as kind as possible. "I know you mean well, but those words don't help."

That rarely seems wise to me. If we try to explain how utterly useless the words are, we may cause offense. These friends are trying to help. If we focus on that thought, we can work through some of the inappropriate verbiage.

One time a man told me that it wasn't the end of the world when I was going through a difficult time. "That's how it feels," I said. "How do you know it's not the end of my world—the world as I know it now?"

What a mistake I made! Not only was I having a difficult time, but that sent him into a kind of pseudo-theological-psychological lecture that left me angry and hurt.

We can skim past such remarks if we consider the motivation behind others' responses and our own. We can assume they want to be kind and helpful. They may be at a loss for words. For us to snap back may bring hurt to them. "Be tenderhearted . . ." we are told in Ephesians 4:32.

We can't dictate others' behavior, words, or thoughts; we *can* excuse them for their insensitivity.

It helps me to think of it this way: *they* want to feel better. They're trying to find appropriate words because they're uncomfortable with their feelings. If we think of our comforters as kindly intentioned, it makes a difference in the way we respond. After all, they don't have to say a word. They could ignore us or walk away when they see us coming. They made an effort, and we can accept their words as an expression of their compassion. How much better than to become disconcerted over whether the words feel right to us!

"Rejoice with those who rejoice, weep with those who weep" (Romans 12:15).

God of comfort, thank you for people who try to comfort me, regardless of how inept their expressions are. Let me hear their hearts and their words. Amen.

Healing Touches

I once worked at a local hospital as a voluntary chaplain. I visited people who listed no church affiliation but said they would like to speak with a chaplain.

When I walked into the room and saw the woman with her skin drawn tightly over her face, I stared for a minute. I recognized her condition as an advanced case of scleroderma.

"Don't be afraid to touch me," she said. Then I did an impulsive thing. I hugged her—very gently. She smiled and said, "I don't remember the last time someone did that."

We've long recognized that patients need physical touch. They call it skin hunger—a need for another human being to touch our skin. We have an inborn need for touch. These days, we're learning to touch the sick, especially the long-term sick, as a way of saying, "You're alive and I recognize it." There is healing in that touch—the connection that says, "You're a real person, and I care about you."

The need of infants to be touched is well documented, and we know that they can die if not touched and held. When we are caring for those with long-term illnesses, we need to find ways to meet their skin hunger, even if they don't ask.

Dianna said that she makes it a practice to hold her father's hand when she talks to the semiparalyzed man. "I often share my news of the day with him. I sit directly across from him, take his hand, and look into his eyes when I talk."

She added, "You know, it's strange, but somehow my taking his hand and focusing on him has bonded us as never before. Dad and I got along all right before, but nothing was special between us. Since I started holding his hand, I've felt connected to him in a way I never felt before. He needs that, and I discovered that I need it too."

Caregivers also need that healing touch. They need to have their skin hunger satisfied as well. Some people shy from hugs or touching, and we need to be careful not to violate their boundaries. Yet many of those who give long-term care need someone to touch them—just a pat on the shoulder, anything to make human contact.

When talking with Dianna about touch, she said, "You know what I've thought about doing? I'm too shy, but I'd like to print a big sign by the front door for visitors. In foot-high capital letters it would read, HUG ME! I LIKE IT."

Although I doubt that most caregivers would resort to making signs, it might be a good idea. (Dianna did buy herself a tee shirt with the words printed on it, "I'm huggable.")

"Some people never got the message, of course, but some did." She also said that she used to be rather shy around people. "Now I've learned to reach out to people for hugs. I've even asked them." She laughed. "No one has turned me down yet."

"And there was a leper who came to him and knelt before him, saying, 'Lord, if you choose, you can make me clean.' He [Jesus] stretched out his hand and touched him, saying, 'I do choose. Be made clean!'" (Matthew 8:2–3a).

Compassionate Lord, sometimes I feel alone and empty. Send those people to me who aren't afraid to touch me and show that they know I'm alive—and hurting too. Amen.

Healing the Memories

Lin had read a book about healing the memories of childhood; she also attended an all-day seminar on the topic. "I thought it was all taken care of and my childhood pain was gone," she said. "Then Daddy came to live with us. That's when I knew the pain-filled memories were alive—buried deep, but very much alive."

Her story has been told by hundreds of other women. When she was a child, her father drank heavily at times. When he did, he became verbally abusive. Her mother cowered from him and never did anything to protect the four children. He once beat Lin's older brother with a broom and broke the handle on the boy's legs.

The worst memory for Lin happened when she was thirteen. Her father picked her up in front of her mother and said, "I'm sleeping in Lin's room tonight." It happened twice after that. Lin ran away from home. Authorities brought her back, but she couldn't bring herself to tell anyone about the sexual abuse, although she did talk about the beatings.

Just before she graduated from high school, her father left them, and she never heard from him again until she was in her thirties. "I've changed," he said, and asked to be part of her life again.

For the next fourteen years, he visited her and her family. Looking back, Lin realized that she always made sure she was never alone with him. "When we were together, I felt like that thirteen-year-old girl again. He scared me, even though my head said that was crazy."

Then came his sickness. "You're the only one in the family who will speak to me," he said. "I've tried to make amends, but they won't forgive me." He was alone, his health was gone, and he had nothing saved for retirement.

His Social Security benefits hardly gave him enough to live on.

Lin and her family took him in. Dad was physically unable to hurt her. His emphysema had worsened so that he was on oxygen. He'd spend most of his waking hours staring blankly into the TV screen. On good days, he whittled whistles for his grandchildren.

"One day I passed Daddy's chair, and he reached out and touched me," Lin said. "I pulled back and screamed. He apologized for startling me, but both of us knew it was more than that."

She left his room as soon as she could. "I ran into my bedroom. I fell on the bed and wept. The memories came roaring back. I had felt that same hand grab me as if I were thirteen again."

For perhaps an hour, she wept and remembered. She prayed for God to help her forgive and forget, but the memories didn't go away. When Lin's husband came home, he held her as she sobbed through the painful stories of childhood.

Her husband wisely didn't try to tell Lin what to do, because he didn't know. He was, however, ready to eject the father. "No, we can't," Lin said. "I don't understand this, but I believe God wants him here. I need this to find true healing for my past."

The next day, Lin confronted her father with the abuse of childhood. At first he denied it happened, and then he made excuses. Finally he said, "That's all past, can't we just forget it?"

"We can't forget it," she said. "I wish I could. I thought I had."

For almost a week, they barely spoke to each other. One day, her father said, "It's all true. There are other things I remember only too well." Lin sat across from him and listened. For the first time, her dad didn't blame anyone else or minimize his wrongdoing. "I'm sorry," he said.

He stretched out his hand to her. It took her a long time before she took it. In Lin's mind, that moment was the beginning of the healing of the past. Lin's father is still alive after more than a year in their home. Their relationship is slowly progressing.

Lin is one of the fortunate ones. She has had an opportunity to confront her abuser, hear him ask for forgiveness, and finally offer it. Every caregiver isn't that fortunate.

The nature of the parent's abuse doesn't matter—emotional, verbal, physical, sexual, or a combination. Abuse is wrong; it scars the souls of its victims; and it doesn't just go away.

Unquestionably, forgiveness is difficult. It's even more difficult when we don't hear a confession. It means having to forgive without being asked, without seeing or hearing repentance. It means forgiving so that *we* are healed.

"I must have prayed for both my parents for months before I could finally forgive them," one woman said. "Even when I tried to talk to them, they wouldn't listen."

In our role as caregivers, we can learn to forgive. When we're ready to open that door and walk through it, we can do it. We do need to forgive—not so much for the offender, but for our own inner peace, our own growth, and our moving forward with God.

"As God's chosen ones, holy and beloved, clothe yourselves with compassion, kindness, humility, meekness, and patience. Bear with one another and, if anyone has a complaint against another, forgive each other; just as the Lord has forgiven you, so you also must forgive" (Colossians 3:12–13).

Forgiving God, help me. Enable me to forgive and to put away the past and be set free. Amen.

Remembering

"I must have heard the story about the swimming accident five hundred times," Lennie Hays said. "It got so that just about every day, she'd tell me that story. At first, I'd say, 'Momma, you told me that before.' She'd say, 'Oh, did I?' and then she'd go on telling it again anyway."

"What did you do to change or resolve the situation?" I asked.

"It really just happened without my figuring it out. I was going through some of her things one day and came upon an old photo album."

Lennie's mother saw what she was looking at and recognized it. "Oh, bring that to me."

They began looking at the pictures together.

"Who's that, Mama?"

For several minutes, Mama would explain about an uncle, a cousin, a teacher, or the pastor of her childhood church. Lennie learned a lot about her mother's troubled upbringing and the many family hardships. Most of the stories Lennie had never heard before.

Lennie had, for instance, always wondered why she was an only child. She learned that her mother had miscarried four times. "That's why you're so special, honey," her mother said.

After that, Lennie tried to find time every day to sit down with her mother and page through the album. All the pictures were old, and Lennie didn't know many of the people, but that didn't matter. Something about her mother remembering and relating the stories bonded the two women.

Others I've spoken with have told me the importance of finding things from the past to talk about. "Maybe when you don't have anything in the future to look forward to, the past looks pretty good," said one man.

That remark stayed with me. It made me think of the Israelites after they had left Egypt under Moses' leadership. For forty years, the Bible says that they wandered around before going into the Promised Land. Some of those people became discouraged. All of them who were adults when they left Egypt died before entering the land. God provided nourishing food and water for them during those years of wanderings. They didn't have to plant, weed, or sow—just go out in the mornings and pick the new-fallen manna.

What did they think about? *They remembered Egypt.*

They didn't talk about the hardships, the long work hours, the cruel treatment. The Israelites complained:

> "If only we had meat to eat! We remember the
> fish we used to eat in Egypt for nothing, the
> cucumbers, the melons, the leeks, the onions,
> and the garlic" *(Numbers 11:4b–5).*

They had been slaves, but that didn't seem to be their focus. Their minds dwelt on the good food of Egypt. Maybe that's the way it works as we age. We look backward, and the old takes on a stronger, more powerful picture for us.

I remember the insightful words of former missionary George Lindsay. After he had been gone from Kenya nearly a decade, he said, "The longer you're away, the more you remember positive things and the more you forget the negative."

I wonder if that's not part of the aging process, too. We know the past because we've experienced it. Somehow our selective memories push away the heartaches and disappointments, and we remember the good times. Maybe that's what happens with many aging people. The past is secure. They can focus on pleasant thoughts.

Perhaps it's also a way to prepare to leave this life. Those final days can be a time for the caregiver to learn and to interact. Even if a parent's mental capacity has diminished so that he or she doesn't recognize you, a picture or a memento from the past may be a reminder.

One woman told me that she displayed pictures all over the house. When she felt tired or discouraged, she'd walk up to a photograph. For instance, she'd see one of herself standing alongside her father's old Chevy truck. There were pictures of vacations when the family went west one summer and another time when they went to Florida.

I heard about a beautiful experience from a writer named Ora Lee. She urged her aging mother to record her memories. "Don't worry about order. Just tell me stories." Several times a week she would set up a tape recorder and let her mother talk. Occasionally, she asked, "When was that?" or "Where did you live then?" Mostly she listened.

Ora Lee said that no matter how much pain her mother endured, on taping days she always seemed in better spirits and complained less of hurting.

"The best part is that it bonded us." She paused and smiled. "I guess that's the word. Mother and I hadn't gotten along well since my high school days. It was a chance for us to reconnect."

Ora Lee laughed self-consciously. "You may not believe it, but I learned to love her during those days. She had such a hard life, but it was so rich. I was glad to have been able to share part of it."

"Bless the LORD, O my soul, and do not forget all his benefits—who forgives all your iniquity, who heals all your diseases, . . . who satisfies you with good as long as you live" (Psalm 103:2–3, 5a).

Generous God, help me always to remember the good things you have done for me as previews of what you will do in the days ahead. Amen.

PART TWO

Practical Caring

Professional Disagreements

During the last year of Edith's life, I became aware there were times when we disagreed with the professionals. Usually the disagreements were over small things, but we had to make decisions about our approach to Edith's care.

For instance, shortly after Edith entered the skilled nursing facility, she was given pain medication only every six hours. On many days the effects had worn off after four hours. "She needs medication more often," Shirley said to the nursing staff. "She's in pain. Can't you see that?"

The nurses, obviously following orders, explained that they could not give her pain pills without authorization. The charge nurse called the doctor's office and left a message. To her credit, Shirley said, "That's not good enough. I'll call myself."

As soon as she came home, Shirley called the doctor. When told that the doctor was busy, Shirley asked when she would be free. Without sounding angry or aggressive, Shirley made it clear that she was going to continue calling until she spoke with the doctor. She explained the reason and said, "I want her to have pain medicine more often."

Two hours later, the doctor called Shirley and explained the side effects of too much medicine. "Wait a minute," Shirley said. "Forget side effects. Forget about her becoming addicted. Edith is dying. She hurts. Isn't keeping her comfortable the most important thing right now?"

The doctor consented and upped the codeine.

That wasn't the only time we had professional disagreements, but it was probably the most significant. We decided something quite early in our caring for Edith. First, we would listen to whatever the professionals said. They were the experts, and we chose them. Second, we would evaluate their instructions. We lived with Edith, and we knew her better than they did.

In talking to people who give long-term care, I've realized that such disagreements are not only common, but they are probably inevitable. Who knows a person better than the caregiver? Doctors, nurses, and physical therapists are trained professionals, but they don't know the individual as well as the caregiver does.

Some caregivers hesitate to complain. Or they complain to their friends, saying, "The professionals know more than I do, but I just don't feel they're giving her the right care."

Here's one piece of advice I offer to caregivers: Don't complain to friends unless you just want sympathy. If things are not the way you think they should be, complain to the person who can rectify the situation. If a home-care worker is habitually late, speak to that person's supervisor. If the food is cold at the nursing facility, complain to the dietician or find out who is responsible.

Act firmly but without anger. Some people assert themselves only when their anger overpowers them. Those who have been around such situations say that boiling with rage rarely works. Angry individuals need to vent their feelings, but they often say too much. They may intimidate or cause anger in response—even when the anger is not outwardly expressed. I urge people to save their outright, expressed anger as a last resort.

"Move up the ranks until you find the right person," said one woman who has had a mother in a nursing facility almost nine years. "Be persistent but stay pleasant. You're talking to other human beings. Approach them as confident, helpful people who work because they like their jobs. You can make their load easier if you handle your concern correctly."

Another person said, "I pray a lot before I make any complaint. I examine my heart and ask, 'Is this something that's minor, something that won't happen again?' I can learn to overlook trivial things."

"Choose your battles," said my friend Oliver. "If you fuss over little things or disagree with the doctor's every word, you get branded as trouble. Then when serious things need attention, you may not get heard."

One thing even the shyest caregiver needs to remember is that by definition caregiving implies being responsible. The title "caregiver" puts that person in charge of the sick person's health. When the health and well-being of a loved one runs counter to a professional's directive, that's the time to speak up.

As one doctor said to me, "The patient's needs come first." As caregivers, we may need to assert ourselves to see that it happens.

"Search me, O God, and know my heart; test me and know my thoughts. See if there is any wicked way in me, and lead me in the way everlasting" (Psalm 139:23–24).

God of wisdom, help me stand up for myself and for my loved one when it's the right thing to do. Help me know when it's purely my own anger or self-interest and when I need to act. Amen.

Three Crucial Documents

"I can't ask her to sign a will," Lori said. "I mean, as soon as I do that, I'll be saying that she's going to die." Lori decided to wait until her mother brought up the matter. That was at least two years ago; her mother has never brought up the matter.

I think Lori was wrong. A final will is one of the three important documents caregivers need. States have differing laws, so it would be worthwhile to consult a lawyer if there is the remotest chance of anyone contesting the distribution of the loved one's property and personal belongings. I've seen some families—including my own—where the death of the second parent brings out every old bruise and hidden rivalry. One way to fight old battles, on a subconscious level, is to argue over the disposal of the worldly goods. The will settles the issues. Siblings may later argue about the fairness, but the parent's wishes will have been fulfilled.

By asking her mother to sign a will, Lori would have relieved her mother's concern. It would also have given her mother the message that, although they both knew she would eventually die, they were taking an important preparatory step.

Shirley and I faced this situation, but because we're both straightforward people, we had no problem with Edith's will or the other two crucial documents long-term caregivers need. We simply talked to her. I know it relieved her mind immensely. She designated money for the Christian college she had attended, as well as funds for two different missionary organizations. They were to be paid before anything else.

Long-term caregivers also need a durable power of attorney. This designates someone to make legally binding decisions. It includes signing checks or selling stocks, should the person being cared for become incapacitated. Having such a document avoids the harrowing process of going to court to have a guardian named to oversee finances and care.

The third needed document is a living will or a durable power of attorney for health care. This specifically spells out the person's wishes concerning medical care. It names someone to make decisions in case the patient becomes incompetent.

If you're giving care to an elderly relative, you need to know everything you can about that person's wishes. Besides making sure all the bills are paid, you'll want to be certain all legal papers are available, such as house deeds and records of investments. The more you and your relative can discuss and work on these matters early in the caregiving process, the easier it will be for both of you.

In the state where we live, because we had the legal documents, we had no problems in closing bank and stock accounts. For almost a year before Edith's death, Shirley had paid all bills and balanced the checking account. By facing the inevitable early, the leftover business transactions became easier for us.

In addition to handling the legal issues, we talked to Edith about her wishes for her body. She chose cremation. On more than one occasion, Edith spoke of the time when she would not be physically limited; she looked forward to a perfect life of health in her life to come. I truly believe that one reason she could talk freely about life after this life was that she realized she could talk freely with us about death. Because we could face the worst with her, she was able to share her eternal expectations with us.

"So it is with the resurrection of the dead. What is sown is perishable, what is raised is imperishable. It is sown in dishonor, it is raised in glory. It is sown in weakness, it is raised in power. It is sown a physical body, it is raised a spiritual body" (1 Corinthians 15:42–44a).

Life-sustaining God, it's easy to forget that you are with me in dark moments and in those times when life seems fragile. Give me the strength to confront whatever I need to do to make these days easier. Amen.

Money Matters

"More than anything else, it's the financial drain that bothers me," Mary said. "My mother has just moved in with us. Al calls it financial sandwiching."

That's a good term, because Mary and Al are sandwiched between the financial demands of raising a family, preparing for their children's college education, and providing for Mary's mother, who has almost no retirement income.

People like Mary and Al are labeled baby boomers—members of the seventy-six million Americans born between 1946 and 1964—nearly a third of the nation's population. Despite a robust economy, they're feeling pessimistic, scared, and depressed.

"It's not just the problem of providing for our kids' college needs and caring for Mary's Mom. On top of that, we haven't done a lot of preparing for our retirement," Al said. "I'm forty-nine. That means I'll probably have about fifteen years to set up a good retirement fund. I worry that I can't do it."

Al's worry was not about the amount of money coming in. He holds a good position, and Mary's part-time consulting brings in a higher-than-average income. It's the output that concerns them. Like a lot of others in their generation, they've lived high and bought what they wanted. Mary and Al chose the lifestyle that says, "Get it now. Enjoy it now. Pay later"—an attitude contrary to their own parents' lifestyle.

"My dad always said to save the money first and then get what you want," Mary added to Al's words. "We assumed that by the time we had saved the money for everything we wanted, we wouldn't be young enough or healthy enough to enjoy the benefits."

My friend, Rob, also one of those caught between the generations, often says, "I'm spending my kids' inheritance." He adds, and I'm not sure if he's joking, "I'm going to die in debt."

They are typical baby boomers, who wrestle with the demands of the lifestyle they have set up. Who wants to lower their living standards? Mary and Al know they could move into an older neighborhood, for example, and get more house for less money. They have two cars plus a pickup, which they justify by explaining the things they do with all three vehicles.

It's their lives. They have the right to spend their money their way. In making the choices they have, however, the pressure tightens. As they try to prepare for their own retirement years, they're starting to feel trapped. Mary says she avoids thinking about it. "When I do, I get depressed," she says.

Boomers struggle with such responsibilities at a time when job security and lifetime employment with a single company are quaint memories. Many have already felt the effects of companies' downsizing and laying off middle managers, as well as the creation of new industries they don't understand.

"And we've just taken in my mother," Mary says.

Mary and Al need financial counseling. This may be a good time for them to look objectively at their lives. In their sandwich position, they may need to look toward their children's future, but they would do well to examine the present situation with Mary's mother.

They may be able to realize that although money matters, ultimately it's not what matters most. If they're really perceptive, they may realize that, poor as she is, Mary's mother may have found something more important than three vehicles and a large house. She is loved and wanted. Isn't that of greater value?

"Many waters cannot quench love, neither can floods drown it. If one offered for love all the wealth of his house, it would be utterly scorned" (Song of Solomon 8:7).

God of all life, point me toward the things that really matter. Keep them before me as I struggle with day-to-day issues. Amen.

"I Can Do It"

In talking to long-term caregivers, these are some of the complaints I've heard often: "He's always trying to get dressed by himself, can't do it, and then gets frustrated." "She wants to cook a meal and makes a mess. It's easier for me to do it than to let her mess up everything in the kitchen."

After Edith had her stroke, followed by hip replacement and a broken elbow, she still insisted on taking care of herself. As much as possible we allowed her to. Gradually, we took over her responsibilities, from sweeping the deck outside her back door to washing her clothes.

The worst part, I think, came when she could no longer make bread. Edith bought wheat from a health food store, ground it herself, and then used a bread machine for the mixing and baking. She made the bread from memory and hadn't used a recipe in years. Her memory was faulty, and sometimes the bread had no salt. One time, it came out so briny we couldn't eat it. Often the dough didn't rise. Each week, she faithfully baked bread anyway. Most of the time we couldn't eat it.

When Shirley suggested that she stop, she refused. "I'll follow the recipe closely next time."

The bread didn't improve. Finally, she couldn't physically get up and do the work, so that solved it. As I've thought of Edith, I suspect that most long-term patients have a few things they hold on to. "I can do it," they say.

It becomes, for them, the last vestige of independence. They can no longer do certain things for themselves. We can't do everything for them, but we let them do what we can and then we need to take over and help.

A few weeks before my dear friend Jimmy Elliott died, he said, "I'd lie in bed and think about something simple, like washing my clothes. I was convinced I could accomplish whatever I needed to do if I could just exert enough willpower. I'd push myself to get up and start to work. For a few minutes, I would do fine, but then weakness would force me to quit. I'd think that tomorrow I'd be stronger. For maybe a month, it was like that almost every day. One of the hardest things was to admit that I couldn't do it."

For many, surrendering those final little things—the things that seem so easy and simple—signal giving up. At least that's how Jimmy saw it. "I'm pretty useless to everyone, even to myself," he said.

For people like Jimmy, being productive or being able to do certain things gives them a sense of some control in their lives. I think it also offers them the sense of having value as a person. When they lie helpless and in pain, depression often sets in.

"I'm no good to anyone," gets said more often than most people know. When Jimmy began to speak that way, I didn't argue. I hugged him. "I'm sorry," I said. My words felt empty and weak, but they were the only honest words I could think of.

I wasn't going to tell him that he would get better. He was dying of cancer, and both of us knew it.

At my last visit, he asked me to open his Bible and read some of his favorite passages from the Old Testament and the New. "Read a verse just for me," he said. "Make it something I can think about while I'm lying here."

I read Isaiah 42:6a several times. "I am the LORD, I have called you in righteousness, I have taken you by the hand and kept you." He smiled. Those simple words brought comfort to him.

As I saw the smile on his face, I thought of how little

it takes to comfort those we love. A word. A hug. A song. It's often the simplest things that do it. I realized that even with my theological training, when he hurt there was only one thing that counted. I was one human being who reached out to another hurting human being.

When he could no longer do for himself, I did one simple thing. It was enough.

Jimmy has now been dead more than a year. I still miss him at times. In my worst moments I think of all the things I could have done and the times I could have visited or phoned. Then I remind myself of that peaceful smile. It had been enough then. It was enough now.

"I am the LORD, I have called you in righteousness, I have taken you by the hand and kept you" (Isaiah 42:6a).

God of compassion, I keep thinking I need to do more or I need greater wisdom or deeper knowledge. Help me to realize that I have answered the call to care, and that's enough. Amen.

Not Easy to Live With

Frank lay in bed following a serious stroke, unable to do anything for himself. His speech was badly slurred. He could talk, although it took effort for most people to understand his words.

For two years following his stroke, Nellie stayed on call twenty-four hours a day. She epitomized the faithful wife by limiting her outside activities, always putting his physical comfort first. Neighbors and friends included her children in their social activities. Nellie said that sometimes five or six days would pass before she actually went outside the house.

As Frank's physical condition deteriorated, their savings vanished. With two children still at home, Nellie had to go back to work. After much internal agony, Nellie finally moved Frank into a skilled nursing facility.

One day a friend talked to her about him and how hard it must be on her. She and Frank had been married seventeen years before his stroke. "In some ways it's easier now," Nellie said. "Frank was never an easy person to live with."

"Really?" asked her friend. "That shocks me! I mean, I had no idea. You never said anything."

"Would it have done any good to complain about him?" For the first time, Nellie spoke to a friend about Frank's abusive behavior, mostly his harsh, cutting words. She could never say or do anything that was good enough. He had to win every argument. Words flowed freely as Nellie poured out her pain to a friend. She admitted that for all but maybe the first year of their marriage it had been that way. "The longer we were married, the more abusive he became." She suspected he was seeing other women, but they never discussed it. Her life had been a living torture. "Now I don't have to take his abuse."

"Why didn't you divorce him?" the friend asked.

She shook her head. "I couldn't. I took a vow to God and I had to keep it."

Now Frank lies in bed, unable to do anything for himself. He is well cared for, but conflicting emotions still fill Nellie's heart. It has been a relief to have him in a nursing facility. When she goes home at night, there is peace. No loud arguments. No demands.

"But I miss him, too," she says to me. "When I come in late to a dark house, he isn't there. I remember then some of the good things about Frank. Once in a while, he'd cook something—nothing fancy because he didn't know how. And yes, I think he did it because *he* was hungry and didn't want to wait for me. But he did it."

As time passed, Nellie remembered more and more good things about Frank. The initial flow of anger subsided. However, words spoken to her in heated anger just didn't disappear. But the daily trips to the nursing facility softened her. She began to look at Frank, not just as an abusive man, but as a person who was hurting.

"He hurt, and the only way he knew how to express it was to hurt others," she told me. "It took me a long time before I finally realized that Frank had always been in pain. He didn't know how to help himself. He attacked, which was what he had learned from his abusive father. It wasn't right and it wasn't healthy, but I finally learned to understand."

"Do you love Frank?" I asked.

Nellie stared at me a long time before she said, "I don't know. If you mean, do I feel anything for him—that romantic kind of thing—then the answer is no. I haven't felt anything like that for him for such a long, long time."

We sat in silence a few minutes before she said, "But if you're asking if I care, then I'd say yes. I do care. I'm committed to him. I'll stay with him as long as he's alive because that's what I promised God."

Nellie didn't know much theology, but she was living and practicing the biblical concept of love. The most common word for love in the New Testament is *agape*. God never commands us to feel a certain way—that is, to feel loving. The word refers more to committed, focused caring, and doing the best for the other.

"If you're doing the best for Frank, that is love, isn't it?"

Nellie wanted to believe my words. She wanted the assurance that she was doing not just the right thing but the best thing for Frank. For years she had tortured herself, unable to make herself feel the emotions she was convinced she ought to experience if she truly loved him. "I always thought that if I really followed God, I'd be able to overcome all his meanness and feel loving toward him."

Nellie doesn't have a magic answer, but she does have the right *attitude*. She faithfully visits the nursing facility. At least once a week, she takes their two children.

They will probably never have the kind of healthy relationship Nellie has yearned for, but she does have peace. "I know I'm doing the right thing," she said. "I've forgiven him, and I've accepted that he's a sad, hurting man, and that he's been in pain all his life. I can live with that reality."

[Jesus said] "I give you a new commandment, that you love one another. Just as I have loved you, you also should love one another. By this everyone will know that you are my disciples, if you have love for one another" (John 13:34–35).

God, Creator of love, help me to grasp that you never demand the impossible from me. Enable me to open myself and willingly serve those in need, even those who seem not to deserve or appreciate my love. Amen.

Needing My Friends

For eighteen months, beginning in 1996, I went through a particularly difficult time in my life. It wasn't a "dark night of the soul" experience. I knew God was around—there seemed no doubt—but God just wasn't speaking. I read my Bible, prayed, sang hymns, went to church, but God was someplace else. During that time, friends made the difference for me. I tried to explain what I was going through, and I knew they didn't really understand my anguish. They did understand that I was hurt and confused, and they cared.

One of them e-mailed me a single sentence, and it lifted me immensely: "A friend hears the song in my heart and sings it to me when my memory fails."

In those dark days, I realized the importance of friends. It was one of those few times when I realized that God created us to interact with other human beings. If we're going to be fully human, we have to open ourselves to other people.

That's how it works. We need people—especially those who support us in our difficulties and trials.

When I've spoken to caregivers, especially those who feel weighed down by caring for their aging parents, they confess that they rarely go anywhere. "A social life? What's that?" said one woman who had once been active in the church. "The best social time I have these days is being able to watch a half-hour sit-com without being disturbed by my mother's groans or my kids' whines."

Effective caregivers have a social support system. I say effective, because they have learned—often through isolation—to have others around them. They can be their best when others encourage and stand with them.

They need to know they're not alone. There are people

who care and people who, if invited, will care. Having those people in caregivers' lives usually means they have to make an effort to reach out for support. They may need to say to a few friends, "I need you" or "I need help."

Studies show that caregivers who have social and emotional support are less depressed and have fewer illnesses of their own. I thought of that today when a friend called me about Elaine, a fifty-two-year-old caregiver. Her grown daughter has severe addiction problems, so Elaine has legally adopted her own five-year-old granddaughter. Two years ago, Elaine's mother almost died from cardiac arrest. She either had to move in with her only child or go to a nursing facility. Elaine insisted on taking her in.

In the process, Elaine closed herself off from everyone. At first she continued going to church regularly and one or two social events a month. Her husband agreed to take over one or two nights each week so she could go out. Elaine also had a number of friends she e-mailed.

After a few months, she pulled back. "I'm too tired to go to church," she told her friends. Elaine lost interest in the social activities and rarely checked her e-mail. An electrical storm zapped her modem, and she's never had her computer repaired. She cut herself off from everyone. A year ago, Elaine fell and broke her nose and her left toe. She has been on heavy medication for various infections. Two weeks ago, the doctor put her on ulcer medication.

"Hey, who's homebound here?" asked Sandy, who had been her friend since childhood. "You never want to shop, eat out, or do anything. You've shut yourself away from everyone."

Elaine went through her list of reasons she couldn't get involved with her friends. "Between Mama and the baby, I'm all used up."

"All the more reason for time out," her friend insisted. "Make outside activities a priority. Go to lunch once a week. Call me, and I'll stay here while you take a walk or see a movie."

"I'll think about it."

"Will you talk to me on the phone?" Despite her promises, whenever Sandy called, all she reached was the answering machine. Elaine didn't return calls.

While visiting Elaine one day, the friend said one thing that caused a stir in Elaine. "If I were at home alone and needed help in caring for my mother, would you be there for me?"

"Of course I would."

"Okay, we've reversed it. I want to be available for you."

The situation isn't solved, but Elaine does go out for lunch occasionally. Her friend is pushing her to do something for herself—just for herself—at least once a week. Occasionally she'll take Elaine's mother to lunch or keep the baby. She's trying to be Elaine's friend.

"A friend loves at all times" (Proverbs 17:17a).

"Some friends play at friendship but a true friend sticks closer than one's nearest kin" (Proverbs 18:24).

God of all grace and strength, help me take hold of those extended hands. Help me realize how much I need my friends. Most of all, help me remember that you are my best friend. Amen.

Surrendering Control

"I just can't do all the things I used to." I hear that commonly. It's part of the aging process. A friend at age fifty-nine said to me, "I just realized that most of the career options I've held on to through the years are gone."

My friend, David Morgan, an avid tennis player, said that at age fifty-six he realized he wasn't going to get better. From now on, it would be a decline in his skills— small, but definite.

If we're aware of those small declines in abilities, how much more difficult must it be for those who are now the receivers of long-term care? How often do they consider the way things used to be?

As we age, we constantly find ourselves giving up a little more control over our lives. That's the way aging is supposed to work. We may not like it, but there's a wonderful wisdom in this. As we slowly relinquish control, we face our own mortality. Not everyone can accept the reality ahead or accept that it is inevitable. Those people fight every step of the way.

Today I thought of three highly successful men in their seventies who have not stepped down as CEOs. They own their businesses, and they just can't let go. One of them I know well enough to say that if he turns the business over to his two sons, who are actually more able than their father, he'll feel empty, unwanted, and that there's nothing left for him in life. "I don't know what I'd do," he said to me, "if I didn't have my job to come to every day."

One day he'll have to find out.

Many hang on, if not to careers, at least to little things. Until they're ready to surrender control, maybe they need to have some responsibilities that say they're alive and responsible.

I remember how Edith tried to sweep the leaves off her deck. When she moved in, I had asked her to keep the deck clean. She insisted she could do it.

Shirley and I agreed that as long as she needed to keep doing her chore, we were going to allow her to do it. One day she stopped. She didn't say anything. After perhaps a week, I realized she wasn't going to do it anymore. I took over the care of the deck. Within weeks, she was in a skilled nursing facility, dying of cancer.

One man said that his father kept renewing his driver's license, even though he was wise enough not to drive again. "Something about the plastic card must have said that he still had some choices in life."

Another woman kept her car in the driveway and refused to sell it. She sometimes got inside and started the motor, but that was all. Her daughter said she'd smile as if to say, "See, I own a car. I can leave whenever I want."

"They don't want me to keep flowers in the window," Mary Ridgeway complained after her first week in a registered home-nursing facility, "and I can't figure out why." She protested against their not providing a remote for her TV. "I can't be yelling for someone to come in and change channels."

Her complaints had nothing to do with flowers or TV. They had to do with surrendering control. For Mary, not to make simple choices about the one room in which she lived twenty-four hours a day signaled the end. As long as she had control over a few things in her life, minor though they were, she was still alive and in charge of her life.

In the end, control does come down to little things—the inability to embroider, paint, read, garden, or play the piano. People clasp those tiny bits of control, fearing that if they release them, they're surrendering and shutting down.

At such times, more than any other, caregivers need to offer assurance that God is there. Their loved ones need reminding that each step forward is also a step guided by God's loving care.

"Where can I go from your spirit? Or where can I flee from your presence? If I ascend to heaven, you are there" (Psalm 139:7–8a).

God of all power, thank you for helping me surrender a little at a time. As I see my loved ones surrendering control, remind me that this is their preparation to be with you forever. Amen.

Testing Sibling Relationships

When it became apparent that Mabel would have to bring Mom into her home, she phoned her brother and two sisters. One sister couldn't make the trip but begged to be kept informed. "I'll support whatever you do." The second sister lived at the far end of the state, more than two hundred miles away, but she came. The brother flew eight hundred miles to meet with them.

The three had an emotional meeting. They all knew that Mom would eventually need someone's care. They hugged, they cried, and they laughed about some of the family's past experiences. They even prayed together for strength and guidance.

"We're with you," they said to Mabel, and they meant it. She was the only one able to take care of Mom. They promised to help out financially from time to time.

All of them agreed. Family solidarity. They loved Mom and wanted a united front in caring for her.

On the occasional visits, the siblings made small remarks. Mabel interpreted them as snide and petty, but mostly she ignored them. These are my siblings, she reminded herself. She assumed that their unkind remarks were their way of expressing guilt for not doing more or taking Mom into their own home.

The situation worsened.

Their weekly phone calls began to irritate Mabel. If she told them what was going on, they responded with, "Whatever you think is best; we're with you." Afterward they often said, "Yes, I agreed, but I didn't think it was going to amount to this."

If she didn't tell them beforehand, they said, "I wouldn't have agreed to that" or "I think you should have done it differently."

Mabel hardly knew what to do. They were her brother and sisters. She loved them and knew they loved her. Aside from sibling rivalry as kids, they had always gotten along. Their criticisms (as she now understands them) began to hurt.

One time in a family conference call, she cried out after a long barrage of what she perceived as harsh criticism, "If you don't like it, one of you can take her."

Quickly, they let her know they thought she was doing a wonderful job. "I just wanted to offer a few suggestions," one sister said.

Regularly, Mabel had to make decisions about her mother, and conflict erupted again. Some of them were genuinely differences of perspective, but there were probably other issues involved as well.

When the four siblings did come together, it seemed to Mabel that they reverted to their childhood relationships. The brother received the most attention because he was the only boy. One sister got away with things because she was the oldest. The baby sister expected others to give in to her. Mabel, the observer and negotiator in childhood, seemed destined for that role again.

For almost a year they fought among themselves, and their arguments went back thirty years. "You were always the selfish one," the baby sister accused the older.

"You were always the one with the big mouth," she responded.

Other accusations went around. Finally, the brother said to Mabel, "You tried to act as if you always knew what was best for everyone in the world."

"That describes you as well," said the older sister.

"Stop!" Mabel said firmly. "Not another accusation."

They stared at her in stunned silence.

"Mom is ill. Her disease is worsening, as we all knew it would. If I am to remain her primary caregiver, I'm going to make decisions, and you're going to have to back me up."

"We have no word in this?"

"Yes, you do. You can offer suggestions. I promise to listen, but I make the decisions." Before they could start arguing again, Mabel said, "If you don't like the choices I make, then you may take over. I'll gladly put any of you in charge of Mom's care. But if I'm the one who lives with her every day, ultimately I will make the choices."

Mabel finally got their focused attention. In a quiet voice, she explained that they couldn't resolve the issues of childhood. Right now, it didn't matter who Mom loved most or who worked the hardest. Mom was terminally ill and would probably live only another year at most.

"Mom and her health—that's what we concentrate on. The arguments and rivalries among ourselves can wait," Mabel insisted. "I don't have the energy to solve them."

Before they went home, they had a group hug. Each of them pledged firm support for whatever decisions Mabel made. To their credit, they did stop fighting. At times the truce tested their relationships with each other.

In the crucial moments, if family members can remain united, the primary caregiver feels supported. That solidarity enables that person to cope and make decisions. It's not always that simply resolved, but when siblings work in harmony, life gets easier for everyone involved.

"How very good and pleasant it is when kindred live together in unity!" (Psalm 133:1).

God of harmony, give each of us peace with each other. Remove our rivalry, and help us unite in this difficult time. Amen.

"I Can Handle It"

"I can do it by myself. Just be there if I need you," Alice told her two sisters. That was a mistake.

They interpreted her words to mean, "I can handle it, and I don't want you to interfere." Alice may have meant something like that. After all, everyone in the family acknowledged her as the nurturing one.

What Alice hadn't counted on—and few long-term caregivers do—was the enormous strain on her physical and emotional resources. "It's not like renting a room to a stranger," Alice said. "This is my mother. I have to take care of her. And caring for her means letting other things go." She smiled sadly and added, "There is only so much of me to go around."

Although Alice didn't say so, she wished her two sisters would visit more often. Both lived in nearby cities. It would have entailed some inconvenience to make weekly trips, but they could have rearranged their schedules.

Alice never asked.

Then her mother went into the hospital. That called for serious decision making. If Alice chose, upon discharge, the hospital would transfer her mother directly to a nursing facility. Should she take her mother back into her home and then, months later, get her on the waiting list for a skilled nursing facility? For the first time, Alice didn't know what to do. She phoned her siblings, and they came together for a few days.

When they spoke about their mother going back to Alice's house, she said, "I can do it," and that seemed satisfactory at first.

"Are you sure?" her sister Gladys asked. Before Alice could protest further, Mona, the third sister said, "I think we need to talk seriously about this."

They met with the hospital administrator, the administrator of a nursing facility, their mother's primary care physician, and their mother's pastor.

By evening, three exhausted sisters had amassed a lot of information. More forcefully than ever, they knew the seriousness of their mother's health. Although their mother had bounced back from other problems over the years, the doctor said, "This time she won't jump back. She's winding down."

As the three walked out of the doctor's office, Mona spoke first. "We need some kind of agreement," Mona, the efficient businesswoman, insisted, and the other two agreed. The next day they met with the pastor and a therapist because they wanted input. They also wanted someone to keep them focused on their mother and not on each other.

"I can do it," Alice must have said half a dozen times. All of them were kind in their response, but they made it clear they felt that Alice could no longer do everything alone.

"Your mother bore three girls," the pastor said directly to Alice. "Don't cheat your sisters out of the opportunity to be part of this."

For more than two hours, each sister presented her perceptions and suggestions. Old rivalries threatened to break in, but the pastor and therapist stopped them when they neared the precipice.

Their concerns, discomfort, love, and even their fears seeped out. But they held to their purpose. Twice Gladys said, "I don't think you're listening to what I'm trying to say." They had agreed in advance that if anyone felt unheard, it was her responsibility to speak up.

"Think of this as a process," the pastor said. "Just getting together and admitting that you need to work together is an accomplishment in itself."

Alice had the most difficulty. She needed help from her sisters and found it difficult to admit it. She had insisted she could do it alone. Until now she had felt more capable than the other two to carry the whole burden, but responsibilities had gotten too heavy. She needed relief, and her sisters not only wanted to help, but insisted on it.

The other two lived miles away, at least an hour's drive, but that wasn't the most important thing. "I don't have to do it alone anymore," Alice said, and tears streamed down her face. "I don't have to be strong anymore. I can lean on my sisters and accept that they want to help."

"Bear one another's burdens, and in this way you will fulfill the law of Christ" (Galatians 6:2).

Caring God, why do I think I can go it alone? Why am I so stubborn that I act as if I'm able to do everything? I need you. I'm also growing more and more aware that I need the helping hands and warm embrace of others. Thank you for teaching me. Amen.

Letting Others Help

"I got so tired of people asking me to let them know if there was anything they could do," Pauline said. She used to smile, thank them, and forget it. If they wanted to help, they'd offer without my having to tell them, she thought.

There are people, of course, who say those words. Perhaps they mean it but don't want to be inconvenienced. Most long-term caregivers have faced that.

Once when Edith was still in our home, Shirley went to a three-day conference. I encouraged her to go. The day before she got back, Edith developed diarrhea. She was so modest she refused to allow me to clean her. What could I do? I couldn't allow her to lie there for twenty-four hours.

A nurse in our church had once said, "If you need anything—anything at all—call me." I took her at her word and called. She meant that she'd make phone calls or cook food. She didn't refuse to come, but I got the message: What she had said had just been words.

By then, Edith had lain in her own waste more than an hour, and I was on the verge of saying, "Forget modesty." Then I thought of Tillie Sandow and called.

She said she would come immediately. I'd like you to know that Tillie has an invalid husband and has been a full-time caregiver for years. I don't know how she does it, but she does get away a few times during the week. She attends church regularly and visits sick people. She had visited Edith more than any other member of the congregation.

Tillie also called the pastor's wife, and they arrived together. Between the two of them, they cleaned and bathed Edith and changed her bed linen.

Too many caregivers don't ask for help because they're afraid of getting rebuffed. And that may happen. Or they can take a chance and ask, as Eve did.

Eve's mother became her responsibility. As a single parent, Eve has several physical problems herself and wasn't sure how she could cope. She's part of a women's Bible study group, so she talked it over with them.

With their help, once a month they asked people in the church (as well as friends and relatives from a list Eve had given them) to sign up for one to three hours of care-giving time.

From her church, a group of women cooked two meals a week, and others volunteered to bring it. Four men in the church took over the outside work and saw that her grass was cut. One of them serviced her car.

For almost a year Eve had the help of her church. "That's when I began to understand what the church was meant to be. I used to think it was a place to go and meet God. Now I know it's also a place to go and meet God's people."

Far too many caregivers hesitate to ask for help. "People get tired of doing things for others." Some people do. There are others who don't.

Eve said, "I learned something important. When I didn't share with my church friends, I was cheating them out of the opportunity to care." She became quite good at telling people what she wanted because a number of them let her know they wanted to help.

[Paul said] "I want their hearts to be encouraged and united in love, so that they may have all the riches of assured understanding and have the knowledge of God's mystery, that is, Christ himself" (Colossians 2:2).

All-caring God, when I allow others to care, it reminds me that you care—through them. Thank you. Amen.

Spiritual Healing

"As Allan got closer to dying, he talked more about spiritual things," June Mann told me after her husband had died of multiple sclerosis. Allan had run around with other women, he had been verbally abusive, and on at least one occasion he had struck June.

But when he became sick, he had to depend on her. For a long time—months—she took care of him because he was the father of their two teenaged sons. "I did it, but I didn't like doing it," she said later.

Once Allan knew the end was coming—and he still lived another two years—his attitude changed. As he faced his death, he began to realize how good his life had been. He looked at his wife with new eyes and asked her forgiveness.

That marked the change for June. The level of caregiving didn't change, but her attitude did. She was emotionally there as he went through each step toward facing the end of his life.

"Allan talked more about God in those last two years than all the other years combined," she said. "He read the Bible and when he couldn't read anymore, I read the Bible and other books about God to him." June's friends came and talked to him and assured him of a loving, caring God.

During that time, June was hardly aware of what was going on inside her as the caregiver. She changed. Not only did she forgive him, but she also learned to love him genuinely. "I saw his helplessness, and he was ashamed of that," she said.

Slowly, it became clear to June that Allan had always feared being perceived as weak. He had to assert his masculinity and prove to her that he was a strong, macho type.

As Allan lay helpless in bed and she had to shave and bathe him, compassion filled her—compassion that she hadn't known she was capable of feeling. In the beginning, she felt as if he were like a hurt dog that needed love and care. But her feelings now went further.

She saw him not just as helpless and hurting, but she understood something else. God loved Allan, and God had "called" her to care for him in his last days. That was the beginning of spiritual healing for June, the caregiver. She once said, "It seemed strange at times, but the more I stopped resenting him, the more he talked about God and the kinder he became."

For years, June had prayed for God to change Allan, to make him into a decent man. She stopped praying that way—partially, of course, because he *was* changing. But even more important, she realized she had been praying the wrong way. "I kept asking God to do something to him. But I needed to learn forgiveness, and I needed the resentment taken away."

June's spiritual healing came slowly. She backstepped and made mistakes, but she kept on. The big moment of her healing journey took place when Buck Maxwell and I came with a portable service for the Lord's Supper. At the end, we paused for a closing prayer. I did something a bit different. I said, "Let's each of us say aloud one or two things for which we're genuinely thankful."

Buck, June, and I all said a few things. I was ready to close when I looked at Allan. With great difficulty, he lifted his hand toward his wife and she took it. "June," he whispered. "I'm thankful God gave June to me."

June cried—the first time she had ever cried in the six years that I had known her. "And—and I'm thankful for Allan," she said. Tears rolled down her cheeks as she and Allan gazed into each other's eyes. I knew that spiritual healing—forgiveness, reconciliation, and freedom from resentment—had taken place.

"Put away from you all bitterness and wrath and anger and wrangling and slander, together with all malice, and be kind to one another, tenderhearted, forgiving one another, as God in Christ has forgiven you" (Ephesians 4:31–32).

O God, sometimes I need healing more than the person I care for does. Heal me so I can be a better caregiver. Amen.

Where Our Mates Fit In

"Things were rough on our marriage for the first three months after Dad moved in," Dot said. "At one point, I was afraid Bruce would say it was Dad or him."

Bruce had agreed that her father needed to live with them. Because of heart problems and diabetes, he needed someone to cook and clean for him.

Time presented no problems because Bruce and Dot left for work early each morning. Dad stayed home alone all day.

That's where the problem arose. Dad didn't have any outside activities. He had no friends in the neighborhood and didn't seem inclined to make any. He showed no interest in joining a senior citizens' group, even though people volunteered to transport him. A group of older adults at his church tried repeatedly to get him to join them for their monthly outings, but he turned them down.

"When we came home," Dot said, "Dad wanted to talk. He had been alone all day. He dozed, read, but mostly watched TV." Dot would have preferred to relax, but she was willing to talk with him.

Bruce, however, came home to relax, not to talk. "Bruce is the kind of man who works hard at his job," Dot said. "He's heavily involved in personnel decisions, and he comes home mentally exhausted. For years, he has set the pattern that when he comes home he needs about an hour to himself without any conversation. He's a private person, and he says he needs to regroup his inner resources."

Dad wanted to talk to Bruce. Dot tried to engage her father, but that wasn't what he wanted. Even when Bruce tried to avoid conversation and acted kindly in order not to hurt her father's feelings, the older man didn't pick up on it.

One time, Dad said to Dot, "It's not as if we're going into any kind of big problems like he has at work. This is just conversation—you know, like any two men do."

Dot's father would begin a long, convoluted story he had heard on the news even though Bruce tried nicely to ignore him. One time he followed Bruce through the house, discussing a rumor he had heard on a talk show about the government cutting social security benefits.

"Maybe we can talk later," Bruce said.

"Yeah, I guess so," Dot's father answered, but he kept talking anyway.

"Just leave him alone when he comes into the house," Dot said. "Don't talk to him. He needs silence."

Her father seemed to understand, and he went back to the TV. Bruce closed the bedroom door. Even that didn't give him the quiet he needed. Because of a slight hearing loss, Dot's father kept the TV volume turned up.

No matter how often Dot tried to stop her father, he seemed determined to engage Bruce in conversation. She tried a variety of things, but none of them worked. She bought a larger TV and set it up at the back of the house, but her dad didn't think the reception was good. She even tried to get him to go across the street to visit an elderly man. Nothing worked.

However, the situation eventually turned out all right. Bruce figured out that getting angry wouldn't help. He also realized that Dot's father wasn't going to change. He decided to drive into the garage and sit in his car until he was ready to come inside and talk. Dot, who got home about half an hour before her husband, always had a pitcher of iced tea waiting for him. Sitting in his car, Bruce shed his tie and jacket, sipped tea, and read.

Sometimes he put his head back and napped. It was his time alone.

Occasionally, Dot's father started to go out to the garage, but Dot stopped him. "No, Dad," she said. "That is off limits until he comes inside."

"Strange way to act," the older man said, although he didn't go out there.

Such situations don't always work out so well. Sometimes the caregiver's spouse can't adjust or resents the intruding parent. "He's more important to you than I am," more than one husband has complained. "If he wants something, he gets it now. If I want something, maybe you'll have time to do it for me later or maybe not at all."

I know of one divorce that occurred over such a living situation. Although the husband had agreed to take in his mother-in-law, he also made it clear that it was his wife's responsibility to care for her mother. He and his wife's mother had not gotten along well before. Their relationship worsened when she came to live with them.

When we bring someone into our home, even an aging parent, we can't make our spouses react the way we want them to. They are individuals with choices just like the rest of us. It helps immensely if we get their support, but they are who they are.

One wife has worked it out that she is the sole caregiver of her mother. Her husband doesn't like her mother. He has said, "I'm not good with elderly people, I'm not patient with them, and I like my privacy." Although the mother eats dinner with them, that's the only time the husband has to be with her. Both mother and husband agreed to the arrangement.

Some may view that husband as uncaring. Perhaps that's accurate. Regardless, he provides the atmosphere that enables his wife to help her mother.

For an aging parent to live in a home and for harmony to prevail, both spouses should agree on their respective levels of responsibility and commitment.

"When others are happy, be happy with them; if they are sad, share their sorrow. Live in harmony with each other" (Romans 12:15–16a, NLT).

Dear loving and caring God, help me understand those who live with me and not demand more of them than they are able to give or do. Amen.

Extended Love

"I hated the idea of my mother going to live in one of those places," Alice Benz said. "It was as if we were giving her up, throwing her out, and crossing her off the family list."

Alice had procrastinated for more than a year before getting her mother into a skilled nursing facility. When the doctors diagnosed Alice with fibromyalgia and the painful disease progressed, she had to surrender. "Not only did I hurt all the time, I felt drained of energy—which I've learned is typical of people with my problem. I finally had to make arrangements."

What Alice hadn't understood—and it was something that gradually became clear—was that the nursing facility didn't take away her mother. Rather, it became an extension of family care. "You may come anytime you want," the head nurse said. They had open visiting hours. Although they refused no one at any time, they requested that family members not come after 9 P.M. or before 7 A.M. "Admission is not a surrender of your rights," she told Alice. "Think of it as an extension of your love and care."

Alice heard the words, but they didn't sink in for a few days. Then she remembered the time she had to fly from her home in Iowa to a nephew's wedding in Arizona. She arranged with a service for someone to come in and stay with her mother for the three days she was gone. The woman cooked meals, did minor housework, and stayed there until Alice returned.

"Allegra (the woman) took care of me. Why, she even likes the same TV programs I do," her mother said. "You couldn't have found a nicer person to stay here."

That was an extension of care, Alice thought. I couldn't be there, so I did the next best thing—I hired someone to take my place. As she considered the present situation, she realized it wasn't different.

"Physically, I can't lift her or do all the things she needs," Alice said. "But they can do it in my place." Alice visits every day. She pulls out her mother's Bible and reads two or three chapters to her. Before leaving, she tidies up the semiprivate room and picks up the dirty laundry to wash at home that evening.

Alice realized that families could view themselves as pushed aside, or the elderly could consider themselves abandoned. It's easier if everyone sees nursing care as an extension—a way to provide the best and most needed care. The facility makes up for what Alice can't do.

"You know the best part of this?" Alice said and laughed. "I can enjoy my mother. At home, we seldom talked. I was too busy doing things and picking up and giving medicine and checking her blood pressure. I don't have to do any of that now. I just sit and enjoy being with my mother again."

On Mom's good days, they talk a lot about Alice's childhood. Sometimes they focus more on watching "All My Children" on TV.

After four months in the nursing facility, her mother said, "Alice, thank you for all the love and care you've provided. I felt so guilty for being a burden." She raised her fragile hand to stop the objection. "I felt I was a burden, and you had to plan your life totally around me. Now I'm being taken care of, and you can take care of yourself. That just may be the way God planned it to be."

"This poor soul cried, and was heard by the LORD, and was saved from every trouble" (Psalm 34:6).

Compassionate God, not only is the nursing facility an extension of my care; it's an extension of your care as well, isn't it? Thank you for providing people and agencies that can help lift the load when we need it. Amen.

PART THREE

Caring between the Generations

Caught between the Generations

The stress of being caught between the generations shows up in many ways.

"I'm such a burden to you," Edith used to say to us. No matter how much we tried to allay her concern, she knew she was a burden. And of course she was in one sense. Her presence restricted our activities. At times, it was as if we had a sick child in the family, because we had to make sure she had her food, bath, and medicine every day.

Shirley and I found it difficult to take vacations because someone needed to be there with Edith. One year, a married daughter left her own family and stayed in our house for two weeks so that we could get away. We traveled with friends in Europe, but we hadn't really gotten away from her. Both of us thought of Edith hundreds of times every day. If an emergency arose, we wondered, how would we get back in time?

That concern didn't occur just when we went on vacation. Like many other long-term caregivers, we (and especially Shirley) realized that being away two hours or going to lunch with a friend didn't mean we pushed aside our concerns. Edith constantly invaded our thoughts.

The sick themselves often recognize the stress they're placing on their families. Going to live with children or being cared for hurts their pride, especially those who have always seen themselves as strong and self-reliant.

"I always vowed I'd never be a burden to my kids," said a seventy-six-year-old man with emphysema. "But look at me now. I walk across the room, go to the bathroom, and come back to my chair and I'm exhausted for an hour." He lamented that now he's forced to rely on his own kids.

In those sandwiching situations, the children of the

caregivers are just as involved, although their parents try to protect them or assume they don't realize the strain. Youngsters know—even if they don't express it in words—because they can feel stress and tension in the house.

Amanda said her five-year-old daughter trailed her throughout the house. "Hold me," she'd plead. "Hold me." Her eighth-grade daughter had complained twice, "You just don't have time for me anymore."

She's right. It saddens Amanda that she can't give more attention to her two children. She can't leave Dad, and yet her pre-school daughter cries, "Mommy, I need you."

"I know I shouldn't resent my grandfather," their eighth-grader finally said, "but I do. When I want a dress washed and ironed for a party, you're either too busy or too tired to help me. You used to have time for me, and now you don't."

Other teens have complained about having to take on extra chores. Their parents told them that having Grandma move into the house would cause extra work. They didn't understand until the situation actually faced them.

Those of the sandwich generation—caught between the demands of their own family members and the needs of their elderly relatives—have no simple solutions before them. No matter which way Amanda leans to help one, she will neglect another. "I feel like a robot at times," she says at her worst moments. "I don't have any feelings or needs. My life seems to revolve around solving everyone else's problems."

When Amanda pauses to reflect, she realizes that her situation isn't all bad. There are conflicts, and she can't please everyone all the time; yet she's also learning that part of her own growth during this period is to face and accept her own limitations.

"Where do I put my energies? my priorities? my commitments? I used to think I could do everything. Now I realize how much I need others and how much I need daily wisdom from God."

Amanda has found Bible verses that help her. When one strikes her, she puts it on her computer, enlarges it, and prints it. Then she pastes it on the side of her bathroom mirror. When she faces tension or confusion, she retreats there. Or she'll listen to tapes from the church service. Occasionally, she has asked a few other caregivers to have lunch together so they can encourage each other.

"I may be caught between the generations," Amanda said, "but I'm not stuck. I see this as God's plan for this phase of my life. As I seek wisdom and strength, somehow I cope."

"If any of you is lacking in wisdom, ask God, who gives to all generously and ungrudgingly, and it will be given you" (James 1:5).

Unlimited God, you have the capacity to care for everyone at the same time and neglect no one. I'm limited in so many ways. As you make me aware of my human limitations, teach me to rely on your unlimited power and love. Amen.

"But I Need You Now"

Seven-year-old Billy called for his mother to find his Nike shoes, which she located in the backseat of the family car. Then he needed her to help him find the blue coat in his closet. Marian Miller, his mother, had just handed it to him when her mother called, "Marian! I'm hungry!"

Marian hurried in to cook her mother's breakfast.

"Mom, I need your help!" Billy yelled from upstairs only a minute later. "I can't find my math book."

"I'm busy right now," Marian called back and continued cooking.

Billy called again as Marian took her mother her breakfast.

In addition to having had a stroke that paralyzed her left side, six weeks earlier Marian's mother had fallen and broken her right arm. She is expected to recover, but for now, Marian has one added task—to feed her mother.

Slowly she spooned food into the waiting mouth.

"Mom! Now!" Marian paused, aware of the frustration in Billy's voice.

"I'll be there as soon as I can," Marian called back.

"But I need you *now*!" He slammed his bedroom door.

Momentarily, Marian closed her eyes. She could envision Billy sitting on his bed, frustration etched across his face. Not being able to find something is his most difficult problem, and it happens about once a week because he's careless in putting things away.

This time his words were the same—"I need you now"—but the meaning sounded different. He had lost his math book, and he would have to leave for school in ten minutes.

The math book isn't his real problem, Marian thought. He needs me. That's the real problem, and I'm not available. But Mom needs me too. Marian sighed, not sure how to respond. After breakfast, she would have to bathe her mother.

"Excuse me," Marian said and left her mother's room. For a moment she paused in the hallway, shaking her head, aware that she stood equidistant between Billy's room and her mother's. For the past eight months, that's been the story of my life, she thought. I've been caught between them.

Tears slid down her cheeks. She couldn't take care of both needs simultaneously. "Who needs me more urgently?" she asked aloud, as she did several times a day. She felt trapped. It didn't matter which voice she responded to. To reach out to one, she had to neglect the other.

"I need you *now!*" Billy called again. "I'm going to be late for school!"

As Marian took the steps two at a time, Billy's words echoed inside her head. "I need you *now!*" For those eight months since her mother had come to live with them, the tension had been growing. Billy needed her; Mom needed her.

Inside the room, it took less than one minute before she discovered the book under Billy's bed. As she handed it to him, she stared into his soft-brown eyes. Impulsively, Marian wrapped him in her arms. As she held her son, floods of guilt engulfed her. She had recently missed two of his softball practices, something she hadn't done before.

Marian closed her eyes, trying not to think of the other activities she'd have to give up in the days ahead. The family didn't go out to eat as often, and she couldn't remember the last time they'd seen a film together or gone rollerblading in the neighborhood. Marian knew it wouldn't be long before she'd hear Billy say, "We don't do anything together anymore."

Sadness overwhelmed her because she realized that it was as if her mother's presence had pushed Billy into second place in her life.

And what about me? she asked herself. There seems to be no place for me. I don't even have time to think about that.

"Honey, I'm sorry I can't do all the things for you that I used to," Marian said and kissed his forehead. "I love you as much as ever, it's only—"

"I know, Grandma." Billy kissed his mother on the cheek. "It's okay, Mom."

As he raced down the stairs, wearing his blue coat and clutching the math book, she felt a moment of relief. The circumstances hadn't changed, but Billy did understand—at least for now.

Once Billy was gone, Marian returned to her mother's room.

"I'm all right," her mother said. "You didn't have to hurry."

Both of them understand, Marian thought. Right now I'm not sure I do. I love them both and want to do the best I can. But some days I'm squeezed between them and don't know what to do first.

As she reflected more she thought, Isn't that how I treat God? I need you now—right now. I don't say it that bluntly, but that's how I feel. Then I get angry when God doesn't rush to me with an answer.

She walked into the kitchen, poured herself a cup of coffee, and stared into the backyard. She couldn't remember the last time she'd done that. But today, she stared at the bluejays fighting with the robins. A monarch butterfly fluttered past the window. "Oh, God, I do need you now. And you are here."

"Ah Lord GOD! It is you who made the heavens and the earth by your great power and by your outstretched arm! Nothing is too hard for you" (Jeremiah 32:17).

My great, loving Parent, I do need you. Sometimes I get so busy caring about others, I forget that I'm as needy—in my own way—as they are. Forgive me. Amen.

Parenting Our Parents?

"Things have sure changed. I'm the parent now, and Daddy's my baby," a weary Melva Paige said to a group of us.

In many ways Melva's father seemed like an infant. He wore Depends because of lack of bladder control. She chose his clothes and dressed him all the way down to tying his shoelaces. With a bib under his chin, she fed him.

"If that isn't being a parent, what is?" she asked.

"I'd urge you not to use those words," Harriette said. "You may be doing the things that parents do for young children, but don't think of it as parenting your father."

Melva thought Harriette was being silly to argue over a term. Jeannie, another person in the group, said quietly, "I think it's important to make a distinction."

"I'm just describing it," Melva said. "And if that's not the correct way to say it, what do I say?"

"Call it long-term care or just caring for him," Harriette said. "You have not become his mother. Look, when our parents are no longer able to care for themselves, we have to accept new responsibilities. Some of those things resemble parenting activities, but I think it's important to keep the relationship clear."

The discussion went on a long time, and it was obvious that Harriette and Jeannie had thought about the issue for a long time.

"Your father is always your father," Jeannie said. "He is not your child." She explained that if Melva called him her child, she would treat him like a child. "That may sound like a mere play on words, but it's more than a matter of words." She leaned forward and touched Melva's hand to show that she didn't intend to sound harsh. "I know it's hard on you, but remember, your father is living with diminished capacity. It dehumanizes him for you to refer to him as a child."

"Those who give long-term care often have to resort to what we call parenting techniques—coaching, pleading, or diverting," Harriette said. "But if we start calling them helpless children we start treating them like children."

"He is your father. He will always be your father," Jeannie said. "Yet there's something more. He's an adult. No matter how diseased his mind (he had Alzheimer's disease) and no matter how little he can do for himself, he deserves the respect given to an adult."

I wanted to applaud Jeannie for her response. I've observed that predicament in many families. It made me think of something that happened in our family. My mother, who was eighty at the time, suffered from dementia as well as many physical problems. She had good days—times of normalcy—but then she'd behave childishly.

One incident in particular has stayed with me. Two of my sisters and I took Mom to eat in a rather nice restaurant. Mom had been fine when we left home, but by the time we were eating, she had gone into one of those bad moments. She became petulant and demanding. Her attitude was about what I might have expected from a three-year-old. "I don't like that corn!" she said. She spilled her coffee twice.

A young woman sitting at the table next to us said to her companion in a voice loud enough for Mom to hear—and I assumed she meant it that way, "She acts like a spoiled child. If she can't eat properly, they ought to take her home and keep her in a high chair."

I stared at my mother, who didn't say a word. She didn't need to. Tears filled her eyes, and she bowed her head. I had no idea what to say, so I reached over and took Mom's hand and squeezed it.

She had nothing to say for the rest of the meal.

Although we never talked about it, Mom felt the sting of those words. I had witnessed the effect of an eighty-year-old being called a child. I wish I could have taken away her hurt, but I could only assure her that I loved her.

I wonder if Mom thought God had forsaken her, as if she had been left alone, unloved and unwanted. Of course, God had not forsaken her. To the credit of my sisters, they had not either. Despite the increasing lapses, both of them treated her as our mother. I was proud of them and their response. She was and remained an adult until she died. She was never my sisters' child.

"I have been young, and now am old, yet I have not seen the righteous forsaken or their children begging bread . . . and their children become a blessing" (Psalm 37:25–26b).

O God, sometimes I behave foolishly or say unkind things. Forgive me. Help me always to help those I care about to retain their dignity. They are adults, and may I remain mindful of that fact. Amen.

"But He Stinks!"

Emily had tried to prepare her three children for their grandfather's coming to live with them. They had family discussions about what it would be like with Granddad there. The children would have to help take care of him. That meant they wouldn't be going away on weekend trips, and they couldn't invite their friends to the house as often.

Because Granddad had lived nearly a thousand miles away, the children didn't know him well. Even so, they accepted his coming. All of them helped to repaint and repaper his room. They seemed excited and told their friends that they were going to have a live-in grandfather.

The fourth day after his arrival, six-year-old Wendy refused to take his breakfast to him. "He stinks, that's why," she said. "The whole room smells like somebody went to the toilet, and it's like that all the time."

Emily did her best to explain about Granddad's illness. "We put diapers on him because part of his problem is that he can't control himself." She reminded Wendy of the time she had had diarrhea. "Well, Granddad will probably be like that the rest of the time he's with us."

Emily and her husband, Brian, tried to change Granddad more often. They used sprays and opened the windows. Sometimes they brought in a fan. The problem is that in his sleep, Granddad pulled off his Depends and badly stained the bed clothing.

Emily tried to talk to the children about the situation, hoping they would understand. "It's something we do because we love him. He's my father," she said.

Little Wendy never stopped complaining about the odor, although she did everything her parents asked.

Other problems came to the surface—such as his

flare-ups of anger over his food and his yelling at the children for making too much noise. He complained when the telephone or doorbell rang. Sometimes Granddad wouldn't talk. At other times, he'd take the hand of whichever child was in the room and talk nonsense. He'd talk nonstop until the child wiggled out of his grasp.

After a few weeks, Emily prayed daily, "God, just get us through this day. Give us whatever strength we need." She knew they all were doing the right thing for him, but wondered why it had to be so hard.

By the fifth month, Emily's patience had given out. The children refused to go into Granddad's room unless Emily or Brian demanded it. The once-close family unit had turned amazingly fragile.

One day Emily poured out her troubles and sorrows to her best friend, Joan. After she had gone through the laundry list of complaints, she brushed the tears from her eyes and asked, "What do I do now?"

"Look, I'm going to give you a verse from the Bible." Joan paused because she was not a person who ordinarily did that. "I'm going to ask you to read it, memorize it, and say it aloud every time you feel like complaining or crying." Joan opened Emily's Bible to 1 Thessalonians 5:18 and read, "Give thanks in all circumstances; for this is the will of God in Christ Jesus for you."

"Are you crazy or something? Give thanks for—for this?"

"No, not for the situation you're in," Joan said calmly. "Give thanks to God in the middle of it all. Focus on the good things in life."

Joan told her friend about a story she had once heard as a child in church. The pastor called all the children forward and gave each of them a dime, pointing out the coin's small size. "Hold it at arm's length and stare at it." They did. "Now move it closer to you." Again they followed his direction.

He had them move it until the tiny coin was about an inch from their eyes. "See! That tiny coin blots out everything else, doesn't it?"

Joan remembered that the point of the sermon concerned not allowing money to become too important. She never forgot the story and saw how it applied to many situations in life. "When I'm in a situation where I think it's the worst possible thing that could happen and everything looks bleak, I think about that story. It's like that one bad thing blinds me to all the good things in life."

"How does that help? What do you do?"

"Once I realize that, I start trying to see other things in life. My way is simple. I hold out my hands in front of me. On my fingers, one by one, I count ten things for which I'm thankful. They can be big things or even small things. It doesn't matter what you give thanks for, just do it."

Emily, desperate for anything to help, tried it. Although she felt no immediate change, she began to make it an ongoing habit. Whenever her nerves tightened, she intentionally relaxed, held out both hands, and silently clicked off ten reasons for being thankful.

One day, the children saw her strange behavior and asked what she was doing. They also wanted to try it. Most nights before bedtime, the parents and children formed a circle and called out. "One. I'm thankful for a nice house to live in."

"Two. I'm thankful for a good Sunday school teacher."

They didn't stop with ten, but kept going until they couldn't think of anything else. Often their list reached into the fifties. The children loved thinking of things to thank God for.

That simple act of giving thanks for specific things in their lives made the next nine months bearable.

Granddad's condition worsened and he died. The evening of the funeral, the family gathered in a circle.

"One. I'm glad Granddad is with Jesus now," said Wendy's brother.

"Two. I'm glad I was able to care for him," said Emily.

"Three. I'm thankful we gave him a home here."

Within minutes they had reached one hundred.

As they prepared for the final prayer, Wendy said, "I'm glad Granddad came here even though I didn't like the stinky part."

"Rejoice always, pray without ceasing, give thanks in all circumstances; for this is the will of God in Christ Jesus for you" (1 Thessalonians 5:16–18).

God of all joy and comfort, help me to realize that there is always joy in every situation, no matter how sad or depressing it may seem. Help me to find ways to be thankful. Amen.

The Child Factor

"I know my children," defensive parents have said for generations. Too often they're wrong. One reason they don't know their offspring is that they don't listen. They assume that just because they live with their children and care for them, they understand how the children feel.

Rather than make such assumptions, why not ask? It's so much simpler and easier for everyone involved.

"How do you feel about having Grandpa move into your room?" That question may not get an honest answer. Sensitive children often assume they're supposed to give the "correct" answer. They don't hear their parents complaining, so why should they? It may take a bit of prompting.

"Since you've moved in with your older sister, what do you miss about not having your own room?"

Once parents give permission, children generally open up. Even young children need to know it's emotionally safe to express feelings. I purposely said *emotionally* safe. Too often children get shamed when a parent says in actual words or by implication, "You have no right to feel that way. If you were a good child, you wouldn't feel that way."

One thing a wise counselor said to me many years ago when my own children were small was that I needed to be careful to affirm my *children and their emotions.* "They need to know it's all right to admit negative emotions," he said. "If they hear a parent tell them, 'Oh, that's silly,' they may not be able to trust their feelings. Don't let them think their feelings are wrong or trivial."

Another thing parents need to do if they also have parents to cope with is to find time every day for the children. It may mean juggling an already overfilled schedule to go to the aquarium or to see a Disney film. Do something with them unrelated to caring for Grandpa. If you don't have a couple of hours, at least make it some time that they know is just for them and for nobody else. After all, you are a caregiver for your child as well as your aging parents.

If your children want to help with your mother, let them do what they can. It makes them feel part of it. Even a toddler can bring a pillow or carry a blanket. One mother asked her three-year-old son to draw a picture of the outside weather every day for his grandmother.

Conversely, accept it when they don't want to help. Don't belittle them. They may be preoccupied with themselves. In their pain or confusion, they may need to distance themselves from the family situation.

If the children develop disruptive behavior during this period, don't focus on the behavior. Focus on the child's need. Children have an uncanny ability to pick up on stress. If the parents feel stressed, the children feel stress as well. They may not know what to do except cry or throw a temper tantrum. Sometimes their misbehavior is the only way they know to get attention. Take all those factors into consideration.

Finally, remind yourself, "I am the parent. I am the adult here." Your child is far less able to deal with emotions than you are. Spending time and talking may help children sort out their feelings. Don't condone the behavior, but accept it. And forgive it.

"I love you so much, darling, but I don't like it when you scream or throw things on the floor. I'm sorry you're feeling this way. Maybe if I hold you a minute, that will help." That sounds remarkably simple. But often the solutions, especially with younger children, are that simple—to us. But they're amazingly complex and beyond the reasoning of the sensitive children.

"Then little children were being brought to him [Jesus] in order that he might lay his hands on them and pray. The disciples spoke sternly to those who brought them; but Jesus said, 'Let the little children come to me, and do not stop them; for it is to such as these that the kingdom of heaven belongs.' And he laid his hands on them and went on his way" (Matthew 19:13–15).

Understanding God, remind me that simple answers work. Help me to listen and to understand. Amen.

Who's Taking Care of You?

Most weeks Christine makes it to our Sunday school class. Sometimes she's just too worn out. A single parent, she has recently begun to care for her aging father, who still lives alone.

Here's the schedule she follows. Her alarm goes off at 6 A.M., and she drags herself into the shower. While she dresses, she calls her father by phone to awaken him, asks how his night has been, and listens to him talk. She goes downstairs and packs lunch for herself and her six-year-old son, assembles the diaper bag for her thirteen-month-old daughter, and cooks her dad's lunch. She also measures out his morning and mid-day medications.

At 6:45 she awakens the two children, sometimes does a load of laundry, and picks up things in the den. Once the kids are dressed and fed, she takes her son to the bus stop half a block away. The bus arrives at 7:15.

By 7:30, she has dropped her baby off at day care and pulls into the driveway of her father's house. Sometimes he's fully dressed, but not often. He moves slowly, for his advanced rheumatoid arthritis makes physical effort difficult. She helps him get his breakfast, puts his lunch in the fridge, sees that he takes his morning medication, and puts his mid-day medicines on the table.

From her father's house, it takes Christine nearly half an hour to get to work by 8:30. This is her "other" job.

She leaves work at 4:30 and first checks on her father. She picks up the baby and then goes to the neighbor who takes care of her son from the time he gets off the school bus until she gets home at 5:45. By 8:30 the kids are in bed, and Christine is trying to unwind while she does ordinary things such as vacuuming, washing dishes, paying bills, and balancing her checkbook.

Christine doesn't date or go out socially. "When I do have time or opportunity, I'm too worn out. The half-hour drive each way is the only time I have to myself," she said once. "And having that time while driving doesn't hold many options."

In those days, none of us in the class understood Christine's predicament. Over the months she didn't open up much. Perhaps a year lapsed before we understood what a hectic life she leads.

Christine knows that thousands of other single parents face similar problems every day. They're overextended and weary. They're on the fast track and don't see any exits up ahead.

"It's mostly feeling that I'm alone and no one cares," Christine said when she and I talked over coffee after church. "I seem to be caring for everyone else. Who cares for me?"

I could have given her the standard answer that God cares; however, I sensed that Christine wasn't asking for information. She had reached the point where she knew she had to do something for herself.

"Who's caring for me?" she asked again, and tears slid down her cheeks. "It's strange, but in the midst of all this, I do know God cares. I'm thankful I still have Dad. I wouldn't give up my kids for anything. It's just—"

The unfinished statement said so much.

Christine has yet to figure out how to sense God's loving arms of comfort around her. She needs encouragement in her dark moments. She yearns for divine strength to carry the load when her arms become too weary to pick up another basket of laundry.

"Have you asked for help?" I finally asked. When she shook her head, I said, "Sometimes we cheat people out of the opportunity to care. How will people know about your exhaustion if you don't tell them?"

Christine finally admitted she needed help. Since then, she's made it a point to have one free evening a week to socialize. It's tough on her budget to hire a babysitter, but it's just one of the things she's learning to do for herself. A neighborhood church has a gym, and she does aerobics while her son is in a children's program and the baby is in the nursery. "Just those few things make such a difference in my life!"

"Depending on others when I can't do it all is tough on me," she said. Christine still struggles, but she's found peace by memorizing and quoting Psalm 23. "Sometimes I close my eyes and see the Great Shepherd holding me closely. Then I know everything's going to be all right. He'll take good care of me."

"The LORD is my shepherd, I shall not want. He makes me lie down in green pastures; he leads me beside still waters; he restores my soul. He leads me in right paths for his name's sake" (Psalm 23:1–3).

God of all care and comfort, remind me that you are my comforter, and you are always present for me. Amen.

Tough Love

"She constantly tried to get my children to do things for her," said Amy Bozeman. "You know, the things she could do for herself and needed to do. She'd ask them to walk across the room and pick up her scissors. She'd say, 'Go get me a glass of water.' Always something."

For six years, Amy kept her mother in her home while she cared for her own five children. The biggest problem Amy faced was not to feel sorry for her mother, not to give in and let her take the easy way.

Her mother needed to keep moving, to stay mobile as long as possible. If Amy relaxed her vigilance, her mother would give up. No discussing, arguing, or pleading made any difference. "She knew she was supposed to move, and she agreed with me," Amy said. "But just as soon as she had another chance to be waited on, she'd take advantage of it."

Today, we refer to Amy's actions as tough love. It maintains that although it's difficult—often painful—to be forceful, we must do it anyway because it's the right thing to do.

We had our own experience with tough love. For most of the six years Edith lived with us, Shirley and I both held home-based jobs. As much as possible, we worked an 8 to 5 schedule. In the mornings before work, one of us would go downstairs to check on Edith and take care of anything she needed for the next four hours.

We encountered one problem: Edith would start talking and wouldn't stop. Most of the time, her monologue went back to childhood or the days before the death of her only son. For the first few days, Shirley stayed there, sometimes half an hour, waiting for Edith to pause, and then she made a quick retreat. Even then, she felt guilty for leaving.

We talked about it. We wanted to care for Edith, but we also had our lives and our work. "I'll go down tomorrow," I decided.

After I had taken care of the normal morning duties, I started for the door. Edith had already begun a lengthy description of something she had heard on the radio that reminded her of something else.

At the door, I said, "Okay, Edith, I'm going upstairs now. Call us if you need us." (She had her own telephone line.) I closed the door and went on upstairs. For the first three or four steps I heard her voice still telling me about something that happened when she lived in Arizona.

All morning, guilt overwhelmed me. I felt I had been rude and mean-spirited. Yet I knew I had done the right thing. Edith knew both of us had work to get out. Had she realized she was hindering us, she would have felt bad about it.

The routine continued for three or four days. "Okay, Edith," I'd say, "I'm going upstairs now." She kept talking.

One morning, however, as soon as I closed the door, she stopped. I had set the pattern. Eventually, Shirley was able to go down, do what needed to be done, and then leave. It wasn't easy for her to cut off one of Edith's long stories, but she learned to do it.

I didn't question the rightness of what we were doing, but I wanted to take my stand with a loving attitude. My emotions didn't always match my action. When I closed the door, especially the first few times, I experienced guilt for doing it and relief at getting away. We "trained" Edith, but I still felt as if I had done something unkind.

In struggling with the tough love issue, I realized that her long monologues irritated me. When she was in the car with us, I turned my mind elsewhere. Many times I asked God to forgive me for being so short with her and for not being willing to listen.

However, I also began to see her compulsive talking as part of her sickness. It was like an affliction, I thought, something she couldn't do anything about. I didn't have to endure the long speeches, but I learned to walk away, to feel more sympathetic toward her. One day I remember thinking, if that was a bad pain in her arm and I had given her medicine, that would be all I could give her. I'd feel sad for her, but I'd also realize that I had reached my limits as a helper. To remain and listen would not have made her healthier.

Just that simple insight enabled me to treat her more gently and patiently.

About three years later, our older daughter Wanda, who lives out of state, spent a weekend with us. She stayed down with Edith for a couple of hours. When she came up, she told us something that enabled us to handle the situation with less stress and more of an assurance that we were doing the right thing.

"I talk a lot," Edith told her. "I know I'm doing it, but I can't seem to stop. I just keep on as long as nobody interrupts me." She told our daughter that I had helped her by cutting her off. "It shocked me, but it was what Cec needed to do."

That awareness amazed us, and my guilt lessened. I had wanted to do the right thing and felt I had done it, although I carried some guilt with it. After Wanda told us what Edith had said, my negative feelings evaporated. In my own way, I had been kind—kind to help her stop talking and not to allow her to go on endlessly. I had been kind to myself so that I could go back upstairs and do my own work.

Sometimes love has to be firm and set boundaries. It had been difficult, but I had done the right thing.

"Love is patient; love is kind; love . . . does not insist on its own way; it is not irritable or resentful" (1 Corinthians 13:4–5).

Kind, loving, and patient God, help me today. Teach me to love with kindness, even if it has to be tough and even if I have to say or do things that are difficult. Amen.

"I Want My House Back"

"These past two years have been tough—really tough," Sally Muse said. "We're barely scraping by. We have two kids in college and two more in high school. Now Mom's living with us. Her pension is so small that I can't afford to hire anyone to take care of her, and she needs a lot of attention."

Sally knows it's only a matter of time before she'll have to put her mother in a skilled nursing facility. She could do it now, but the guilt and the sense of failing her mother won't allow her. So she has another member of her family living with the six of them.

Sally and others have taken on this responsibility. For many of them, taking it on wasn't the problem. They did it because they felt it was the right thing. But once they lived in that newly created environment, the price sometimes got awfully high.

"I'm tired. I'm tired all the time," Sally says. "No matter how much my kids and my husband try to do for me, I always seem to be on the go and I don't know how to stop."

She's not alone.

I sometimes hear a note of sadness from people in their forties and fifties. "We have our own families, and now we have Dad. We expected to take our kids through life, the way Mom and Dad took us. We didn't expect to take in our elderly parents."

It's hard on Sally and Brad, but the children feel the pressure as well. They get a distorted picture of older people. "Grandma gets food all over her face when she eats," they said. "Grandma won't take her medicine unless Mom or Dad is there to watch her. Then she gets sick, and they have to take her to the hospital."

Sally and Brad have had to explain that all older people don't behave that way. Yes, there are problems whenever anyone takes in an older family member.

For instance, Sally has complained, "I want my house back." Her husband wisely understands that this is her way of crying out, "I want life to be the way it used to be. I want some control again."

It won't be Sally's house again for a long time.

Our writers' group used to meet at her house once a month. "You can't come here anymore because Mom has taken over," Sally said. Then she apologized for the way she had spoken, but we understood.

Sally's mother was frail, and her physical problems often required her to spend two or three days at a time in bed. Even in bed, she frequently demanded attention and wanted everything brought to her quickly. When she was up, she wandered all over the place. For the first time in their twenty-three years of marriage, Sally and her husband had to lock their bedroom door to keep her mother out. They had to remember to lock the bathroom door or Mom might just walk in.

"Mainly, it's hard because she's with us all the time. When I finally sit down to watch TV, she's next to me. If I start to watch a program and she doesn't like it, she says, 'Oh, that's such a stupid show. Let's watch something else.' "

Sometimes the TV is too loud and she complains, or it's not loud enough and she can't hear it properly.

Sally admits her house isn't as clean as it used to be. "Some days if I can find a path to walk through the clutter, I feel it's been a good day." Her mother constantly reminds Sally that when she was growing up, she never saw such a mess in her mother's house.

"If I pop popcorn for a snack, she'll say she wants

some and then won't eat any. Or she'll say she's not hungry and then eat most of mine."

"One day I'll have my house back, but not right now," Sally now says. "It's taken me a while to accept that this is the way my life is. Mom is here. She's more important than my house or the way I'd prefer to live."

"You will keep in perfect peace all who trust in you, whose thoughts are fixed on you! Trust in the Lord always, for the Lord God is the eternal Rock" (Isaiah 26:3–4, NLT).

God of all peace and joy, help me realize that the tender care of my loved one is my task now. Give me peace while I do the right thing. Amen.

Being Honest

"Why doesn't Grandpa get out of bed?" "Why is Grandma grumpy all the time?" "Why does she yell at me when I play?"

"How much do you tell the children?" parents sometimes ask after one of their parents has become a long-term patient, usually in their home.

Even small children understand when we give them answers. We don't have to give them complete medical information, but they can understand when we put things in simple terms.

"Your grandfather is a very sick man," is one way to start. "He's in bed most of the time because it hurts him too much to get up." "Your grandmother had a stroke. Something happened to her brain, and she can't move on her right side. That's also why she sounds funny when she speaks."

When we give those simple explanations—even when children don't grasp all the words—they absorb more than we may think. Really, it's not so much whether they grasp the words; it's that they know they're included. They're not just sitting there unsure of what's happening.

Sometimes they need to understand what they're feeling. When children are fairly young, parents need to watch their emotional reactions and let them know it's all right to feel the way they do. "I know you're sad, Jeremy. It is sad to see Grandma hurting like that, isn't it?" "Her words sound awful, and you hate it when someone talks that way to you, don't you?"

Alice Jean said she told her daughter, "Try to remember that Grandpa hurts. He hurts so much, he doesn't realize how mean he sounds. Just go up and kiss him."

The child's simple action worked, and the grandfather explained that he wasn't angry at her.

Honesty also extends to kids and their needs. I recall years ago visiting a home where the wife took care of both her parents, both bedridden most of the time. Her daughter, who may have been four years old, wanted to go outside and play on the swing.

"You can't. I don't have time to push you."

"Please, Mommie, just for a little bit."

The begging persisted until the mother said, "Don't be so selfish! You can play in your room. I have too much to do." The little girl left the room. I'm sure she felt guilty for wanting to play. No child should have to feel that way.

Had she seen the quick flash of pain on her child's face, I'm sure the already-frustrated mother would have broken down into tears. How I wanted to say, "Why didn't you explain? Why didn't you tell her you love her, but you just don't have the time to do things with her that she wants? It may not cure everything, but at least she'll know it's not her fault."

Years ago, I marveled at how the Severin family coped with their retarded son. They encouraged their children to ask questions. I was there when Dawn, the smallest child, asked, "Mom, will Georgie ever walk like me?"

"No, dear, he won't," Edna said. "Something is sick inside him. He won't ever learn to do things you can do already."

"Will he talk? You know, real words?"

"I'm afraid not," Edna said.

Dawn stared at her brother, kissed his cheek, and said, "That's sad. I'd like to have him talk to me."

Openness and honesty—they are two concepts to consider with our children. When we try to hide anything from them, we may be successful, and they may never know what's going on. Most children, though, are immensely perceptive and often know something is happening. Because younger children are egocentric, they may assume they have been bad or they have caused the problem. As parents, we need to make it clear that none of these difficulties are their fault.

One of my friends talked about death to her two children. She wanted to be certain they were prepared when Grandma died.

"Did I do something bad?" her son had asked when his grandmother stopped getting up during the day. "Is she mad at me?"

"She's sick, and she's getting worse," the wise mother said. "It's nothing you or anyone did. That happens to some people when they get old." Then she suggested that whenever possible, he might go into Grandma's room and give her a big hug. "You don't even have to say anything if you don't want to. She hurts, and hugs help her feel better."

"I'll give her lots and lots of hugs," the boy said.

Honesty—that's what works best.

"Even though I walk through the darkest valley, I fear no evil; for you are with me; your rod and your staff—they comfort me" (Psalm 23:4).

God of life and death, help me speak honestly but lovingly. Help me face reality myself so that I can express it to others. Amen.

Compromised Caring

Those who have a strong, supportive home front are truly blessed. Even if family members don't participate directly in the work of caregiving, their supportive attitude and concern is a gift.

"My husband listens to my litany of complaints," Mary Jo Hansen said. "People who haven't been there don't understand how much it helps. Mom is in the early stages of Alzheimer's disease. Once in a while, she does outrageous things. But he's always there to encourage me." As her mother's memory goes, Mary Jo has been told that such things will become more common. "As long as I have my hubby to listen, I can cope."

In many families, having an aging parent means the mate or the children take on extra duties. They give up things, such as privacy and claims on their parents' time. Long-term care of anyone involves compromise all along the way. Households that make those adjustments become stronger in the process.

Others become strained and remain that way for years. One thing I've realized in talking with long-term caregivers is that whatever problems existed before the intake of a relative are exacerbated afterward. The responsibility has sometimes forced the worst part of the marriage to come to the fore. Then the couple must decide if their relationship is worth saving.

"Who comes first in this family?" one husband asked. "I thought you married me and that you left your family to start a new one with me."

When that question (or a similar one) comes up, compromise becomes the only answer for survival of the relationship. We like to think we all have mates who are understanding and supportive. Reality, however, says that some people see themselves as the primary object of care within a home. As long as they are cared for and their needs are met, they're fine. But they have to feel that they are in first place. Unfortunately, this type is rarely ever satisfied and always demands more than anyone can give.

It may be that in such instances, long-term care isn't workable. It may mean that the mate is unable to compromise. Then the choice comes. If marriage is primary and the spouse isn't willing to compromise, the burden can be quite heavy. One couple said, "We couldn't take my mother. Our marriage was just to fragile." The couple did provide financial support for a sibling to care for the mother.

I've seen a few instances, always with wives, where the care of the aging parent becomes all-consuming. When that becomes obvious to the rest of the family and they say so, the caregiver needs to back up. The need may be great, but the caregiver needs to ask, "Who comes first? Dad or my family?" There probably won't be enough of the caregiver to spread around and get everything done.

One wife complained to her pastor about the demands and her being sandwiched between her family and her aging father. The pastor advised: "Your father may have to settle for less of you. Your husband and children need you, even if they don't demand your attention."

If you suspect you're giving too much to your parent, talk to your family. Ask them to help you put the caregiving in perspective. "Mother is important in my life, but she's not all of my life," said Linda. "For years, as an only child, I was there whenever she needed me. Now I have a family, so I can no longer give her all that attention."

"I love you," Linda told her mother, "but as much as I love you, you're not first in my life." Even though she said she understood, it was obvious she felt rejected by her daughter. Those were hard words for her to say, but it clarified the relationship.

By contrast, Ron and Sara Darling said they wanted to avoid a tug of war. They sat down and discussed things with their two teenaged children two evenings before they invited his mother to live with them.

Here are a few things they shared for other families to consider.

First, who is responsible? How much should the other person give up or change to accommodate the new situation? What is each prepared to do, to take on, or to give up?

Second, how can/will your spouse help? For instance, if he or she offers advice, is that what you really want? Or does it upset you and make you feel inadequate? Don't expect your spouse to become an instant mind reader or know how you're feeling. Tell your spouse what you'd like, such as, "I'd like to be able to drop by Mom's on the way home from work. Either we'll have to eat later or you start dinner."

Third, consider your mate's feelings. The stress affects your mate even though you may be focused on your parent. Not only are you giving your mate less attention, he or she also may feel shut out or unwanted, because he or she can't share your pain. Your spouse may be afraid of appearing selfish if he or she voices his or her needs.

Fourth, make time to spend with your mate. When your parent's care is chronic, it's even more important to take time out to be alone with your spouse. It can be a quiet dinner out, a walk in the woods, a long weekend, or a baseball game in another city.

One couple sets aside Friday night as their date night. No matter how tough the week has been with the man's mother, they have their night out. They hire someone to come in.

Twice, the mother has gotten sick and needed them, so they rescheduled their date. For the most part, however: "It's our time. We need each other and we need to keep growing together."

"For you were called to freedom, brothers and sisters; only do not use your freedom as an opportunity for self-indulgence, but through love become slaves to one another. For the whole law is summed up in a single commandment, 'You shall love your neighbor as yourself' " (Galatians 5:13–14).

God of wisdom, I realize that I'm constantly confronted with choices and compromises. Help me make wise choices. Mostly, help me to love and to show that love. Amen.

PART FOUR

Caring and Feeling

Resisting Change

"It seemed simple enough," Iris said. "Mom can't live alone, she needs help, and both of us knew it. She asked if she could live with us."

Iris didn't hesitate. "You're my mother," she said. "Of course, we want you."

Evelyn loved the idea of moving in. Iris was her older daughter, and they'd always gotten along well. Delightedly, she telephoned her close friends to inform them of the change. The emotional high for Iris and for Evelyn lasted almost two weeks. They didn't have a big blowup or loud words, but both of them knew it wasn't quite as good as they had expected.

"If Mom would just change," Iris complained to her husband and her own three children. "She's lying in there, hardly able to walk across the room, and she still acts as if I'm nine years old. She's not in charge now, but she resists changing. Things are different now than they were thirty years ago."

The sadness of the situation is that Evelyn doesn't realize she's resisting or not adjusting to the changing relationship. She can't understand why Iris sometimes turns sullen or speaks sharply. She's not aware of how demanding she is.

One day Evelyn called Becky, her younger daughter. When she hinted that she wanted to move in with her, Becky said, "I don't think so, Mom. I'll help Iris as much as I can, but I can't take you."

Shock filled Evelyn. She wanted to blurt out, "After all I've done for you?" Fortunately, she mumbled something such as, "I'm sorry you feel—"

"I love you, Mom, but it wouldn't work. You and I

didn't get along the last two years I was at home. Why would it be any different now?"

Evelyn talked about changing and growing up. Mostly she implied that Becky had matured over the twenty-five years since she had left home.

"You're my mother and I love you. But you're as inflexible as you ever were. You always have to be right! You're as bossy now as you were years ago."

The words flowed back and forth, and Becky threw the punch that ended the conversation. "We're not little kids anymore, and we're not your personal servants. We grew up. You need to do the same. *Grow up, Mom!*"

After Evelyn hung up, she wept a long time from anger, rejection, and quite a lot of self-pity. Late that night, long after Iris and her family had gone to bed, she couldn't sleep. She started to call for Iris to come in. Then she stopped.

As she lay in the dark, Evelyn realized her worst fear—abandonment. Her own children didn't care, and she feared Iris would get rid of her soon. Her church had abandoned her. In the past eight months, not one person had contacted her. Now that she could no longer go out socially, most of her friends had stopped calling.

"It hurts, God, it hurts," she cried. As tears flowed freely she heard herself say, "I hope they never feel abandoned the way I do."

As she reviewed her own self-pitying words, they brought back a memory of her own mother. "I hope you never feel abandoned the way I do." Her mother had flung those words at her more than twenty-five years earlier when Evelyn had put her in a nursing facility. As other memories forced themselves into her consciousness, Evelyn reflected on how difficult her mother had been.

"Am I the same way? Am I demanding and quarrelsome the way she was?" she asked herself. The next morning she asked Iris.

"Yes, Mom, you are."

"I don't want to be like that," she said. "I—I want to grow up. I want to change. I'm not sure I can, but I want to try."

This story is real; the names are not. Both women are struggling over this. Some days it looks as if harmony will fill the air forever. On other days, fiery words blaze throughout the house. But they're talking. They're trying to be open to each other.

"Maybe I'm growing up," Evelyn said after one of their long talks.

"At times, I still feel like a little girl, and I can't always figure out why," Iris said. "It's just something that clicks in— an emotion from long ago—and I feel powerless and tiny."

Iris told me that it sometimes happens when Evelyn thinks she's affirming her. She'll comment on how well-cooked something is or how nice the house looks. "But the way she says it makes it sound like criticism. I keep hearing the tone of you're-not-good enough. Even though my head says that's not what she means, my long-held inside pain tells me differently." Iris can't always get rid of those memories, but she's working on them. "I'm growing up, too," Iris said.

> "Brothers and sisters, do not be children in your think-ing; rather, be infants in evil, but in thinking be adults" (1 Corinthians 14:20).

God, our heavenly parent, it is hard to grow up, especially once we're older. Even though I sometimes resist, life pushes me toward growth. Help me to see this in human relationships and in my relationship to you. Amen.

Not Being a Burden

"I never want to be a burden on my children." I wonder how many times most of us have heard that statement from parents. They're usually thinking of money. They want to provide for their own financial needs and not have to be a strain on their children.

One woman, who watched her parents care for their elderly parents during the depression years, vowed that she'd never allow her children to take her in and upset the household. Fifty years later, she has to depend on her two married sons. Obviously, it hasn't been easy for her.

"Mama has always valued her independence," said Martin, her older son. "Now my wife and I have to take care of her. I think it's harder on Mama than it is on us."

In some ways it is. His mother believed that the best she could do for her children was to care for them until they left home and then never to trouble them again.

Doesn't it work both ways? Isn't Mama missing out on wholesome interdependence? Does Mama need her sons? Yes, she does.

That doesn't mean she readily admits it. She talks about moving into "one of those full-retirement facilities. As you get worse, they move you into a different place," she said. "I wouldn't like it, but I could do that."

Mama may not want to admit it, but her life is richer for having been with her son and daughter-in-law. It's certainly less lonely. She has family around her. One thing about family is that they learn to overlook peculiarities that might offend or inconvenience strangers.

Mama has had the hardest time admitting that she needs her children. She needs to know that she matters, that they want her company, that she's not just a relic that has created a heavy burden on them.

More than once she has said, "Oh, don't bother about me. I can take care of myself."

Despite the firmness in her voice, her children know she can't. They haven't let her get away with such statements. "Mama, we want you here," Martin has said often. "We want to help you."

Despite his deep love, Martin knew that his mother wasn't always easy to live with and could be extremely stubborn. His wife, Betty, knew it as well. Betty didn't work outside the home, so she would obviously have to provide more physical and emotional caregiving than Martin. When they discussed the situation, Betty readily agreed to have Martin's mother move in because she loved her mother-in-law. "She belongs with us."

Martin's mother didn't see it that way. Several times she had refused to move out of her own house, even though she increased the worry and anxiety on the part of her family. Martin finally used the weapon he knew would win her over. He took his Bible and went to visit.

"Mama, even if you don't like it, you have to move in. You have to do it because the Bible says so!"

A startled mother stared at her son. She couldn't think of a single verse that said that.

He opened his Bible to Paul's first letter to Timothy: "Honor widows who are really widows. If a widow has children or grandchildren, they should first learn their own religious duty to their own family and make some repayment to their parents; for this is pleasing in God's sight" (1 Timothy 5:3–4).

Martin stared at her. "Did you hear that? He re-read the part, "and make some repayment to their parents."

Although Martin presented it as his repaying her, both of them knew it meant more than that. Mama finally admitted, "It means so much that you want me, that you don't want to push me off into some nursing facility and forget me."

Time is short. They all know that and are making the most of it. Sometimes Betty is worn out (although she rarely complains), but she realizes the importance of the connectedness.

It's hard for some outsiders to understand this connectedness, and it has nothing to do with burdening or being a burden. It's part of the divine relationship God created through families.

I saw this illustrated a number of years ago when Marcia went to see her mother in the nursing facility almost every afternoon. Her mother had Alzheimer's disease and had long forgotten who Marcia was. The daughter kept going anyway.

"Why do you go?" a friend asked her. "She doesn't even know you're there, and she wouldn't miss you if you didn't visit."

"No, no, you don't get it. I'm not going for *her*. I'm going for me. She's my mother. She brought me into this world, and she was there for me every day of my life. I can't leave her now."

In relating this, Marcia finished by saying something that made it clear to me. "It doesn't matter whether she knows. I know. I know I'm there. It's where I belong."

That's the way it works with families. We have some invisible connection that we didn't choose and might never have wanted. But it's there and will be there as long as we're alive. We can choose to honor that connection as Martin, Betty, and Marcia have done.

"Hear, my child, your father's instruction, and do not reject your mother's teaching; for they are a fair gar-

land for your head, and pendants for your neck"
(Proverbs 1:8–9).

Understanding God, many times I don't understand my feelings or my reasons for doing things. But I do understand that Mom (or Dad) is here now. My responsibility is to be here, just as I know you're here now and will never, never leave me. Thank you for that unexplainable connection. Amen.

Crossed Purposes

"Mom needs to go into a nursing home," Sheila said to her two sisters.

"Never!" one of them screamed. "No one's going to bury our mother in one of those hell holes!"

The other sister waffled, depending on who was arguing.

The situation wasn't that unusual. When more than one person is involved, crossed purposes often occur.

When Deanna North's father faced the last days of his life, she and her sister wanted him to go to a hospice. Their brother adamantly refused to give consent.

When Mary Marvin's mother became seriously ill, Mary wanted her mother to go to a personal care facility where she would have other people around her. Her siblings didn't want her to leave her own house.

Crossed purposes. How can that be? If three children all love their mother, why can't they agree on the method of care or allow the one person who's primarily responsible to make the decision? In some families, that's exactly what they do, of course.

Perhaps the issue isn't just the care of the loved one, but something that goes much deeper. Maybe it's an issue about the caregivers themselves.

I saw this after Richard was diagnosed with colon cancer. It had already spread into his spine. The doctors consulted with his wife (whom he had married only two years earlier) and his daughter, with whom he had lived for five years before his remarriage.

The daughter wanted to take the doctor's suggestion and have her father undergo chemotherapy. "We need to do anything we can to keep Daddy alive," she said.

The wife opposed what she called the "prolonged

pain" method. "The most they can do is keep him alive. They can't promise that he'll be healthy again. He's seventy-one, and he's had a good life. Isn't that enough?" The wife had gone through a long ordeal with her first husband, who died of lung cancer.

Both had valid feelings, yet neither could accept the other's position.

They talked to me about the situation. In the two conversations we had, the daughter finally admitted that she just couldn't let go. "I love him. He's been there for me, and we just have to do everything we can for him."

The wife, who had the legal power to make the decision herself, had been through the treatment of advanced cancer before. She only wanted him made comfortable and as pain-free as possible while he awaited the inevitable. The wife could have overridden any objection. "Richard's daughter probably would have given in had I insisted, but I loved her too. I agreed to chemotherapy."

Other families find various ways to resolve conflicts when it comes to care and treatment. Often getting to the solution brings out long-buried feelings of pain, anger, favoritism, and rejection. In trying to discern what's best for the person in long-term care, it's also important for those involved to examine themselves.

When families are at cross-purposes, it can be both a healing and a growing experience if they talk. But talk isn't enough. They may need to examine their own hearts to discern what's going on that separates them.

"Do not use your freedom as an opportunity for self-indulgence, but through love become slaves to one another. For the whole law is summed up in a single commandment, 'You shall love your neighbor as yourself'" (Galatians 5:13–14).

God of all wisdom, so often I don't understand my motives. Grant me wisdom to know what's going on inside me. Give me strength to face my hidden motivation. Amen.

Guilt-Inducing Words

"Oh, I felt guilty a lot," Evelyn Lee said. "There were three words especially that never failed to throw me into depression and guilt." She smiled and said, "But once I recognized them, I started telling people they couldn't talk that way to me."

Evelyn was one of those feisty individuals who had never heard the word *sandwiched* to describe her, but that's what she felt like. Her two sons were in high school, and her mother suffered from angina. The daily trips from her home in Zion, Illinois, to Highland Park took a minimum of forty-five minutes each way. "I was a single parent with kids at home. I had to work yet also take care of my mother's needs."

Finally, Evelyn's mother moved in with them, and she expected life to be easier, but it wasn't. Her mother's condition worsened, and other health problems developed. No matter how hard she worked or what she did, Evelyn felt she was getting further and further behind.

"You really ought to have someone come in and help," one friend said. Evelyn didn't answer. First, she didn't have the money to hire someone. Besides, her difficult-to-handle mother barely tolerated the visiting nurses who came in.

"You should take better care of yourself," said a co-worker. "You look so tired and run down." Again, Evelyn kept silent. How could she take better care of herself when she never had a moment for herself?

"You must be more careful with yourself. You shouldn't give so much of yourself to her."

Those were typical comments from well-meaning friends. They didn't understand the impact of their words. "When they used *ought, must*, or *should*, they had no idea what they were doing to me," she said. "They probably didn't mean those words as strongly as I heard them."

Evelyn's mother added to the guilt. "You should have insisted on my coming here earlier. You ought to have listened when I said I couldn't take care of myself."

For months, Evelyn's head swirled with all the guilt-pointing fingers–or at least that's the way she interpreted them.

In desperation, she went to her pastor, even though it had been nearly three months since she had been in church. He listened silently as she poured out all her woes and especially all the feelings of guilt. "Don't you have anything you can say to help?"

"One thing comes to mind," he answered. "Only God has the right to impose guilt on you. You feel guilty enough by yourself without anyone's help."

She smiled, knowing he understood, and she left with the resolve not to internalize all those *shoulds* and *musts*.

That same day, she was an hour late coming home. During that time, her mother had had an accident. Unable to get to the bathroom in time, she had urinated on herself. "You should have been here," her mother said.

"Don't ever use that word with me again," Evelyn said quietly and began to help her mother clean up and change her clothes. "I love you, and I have brought you to live with me. I'm doing the best I can."

"I know that."

"When you use a word like *should*, I feel ashamed, as if I've neglected you, that I'm not doing enough."

"Well, if you had been here, this wouldn't have happened."

"If you were still living alone, what do you think would have happened?" Evelyn had never talked to her mother that way before. "I'm not your little girl anymore. I'm grown, with my own children. I have other responsibilities in my life."

"I know that!"

"Then don't tell me what I *should* do."

Silence filled the room as mother and daughter stared at each other. "I feel inadequate to begin with," Evelyn finally said. "Every time anyone uses guilt-inducing words, I sink low. If you want me to do my best, don't shame me or make me feel worse."

Mother protested that she had not meant to make Evelyn feel that way. The daughter responded by saying, "It doesn't matter what you intended. I know how I hear it, so don't talk that way to me anymore."

That was the beginning of freedom for Evelyn. When friends gave their pointed advice, she began to stand up for herself. "I feel useless when you talk that way," she said to her neighbor. "And that makes me feel guilty for all the things I don't or can't do."

The surprised neighbor said, "You do a wonderful job, far more than anyone would expect. You have no need to feel guilty."

Evelyn has continued to work on her guilt. Her biggest protection is to refuse to allow anyone to bombard her with the three guilt-inducing words.

"Jesus answered them, 'Very truly, I tell you, everyone who commits sin is a slave to sin. . . . So if the Son makes you free, you will be free indeed' " (John 8:34, 36).

God of grace and freedom, help me. I fail often, and I know you forgive me. Yet deep inside, guilt keeps sneaking in. Help me overcome all those negative feelings. Amen.

PWT

I first heard about PWT when I visited an AA group near Louisville, Kentucky. One woman started talking about how difficult it was to accept social invitations. "All my old friends drink. So far, none of them has insisted I have a drink, but, uh, well, I think about it a lot."

"PWT," called out someone from across the room. Most of the people smiled or chuckled.

"Oh, of course, you're right." She pulled a small notebook from her purse and wrote something on it.

Only after the meeting did I get an explanation from Richard, the man I accompanied to the meeting. "It's short for *Private Worry Time*." He laid his hand on my shoulder and said, "Before you think it's nonsense, I want to tell you that it works. It really does."

He said that throughout the day, whenever the group members became upset or started to worry about something, they wrote key words about the nature of the problem on a notebook, pad, or even a slip of paper. "You see, when I write it down, it's a way of saying to my mind that I've put this on hold until I have my PWT. I refuse to dwell on it, because I can worry about it later." He laughed self-consciously. "Even though it works for me, it's not the way for everybody. But those who faithfully use the PWT find it helpful."

After Richard and I talked a while, he said, "Okay, call it a matter of prayer if you like. That's what it really is. It's just that among us here, the word *prayer* doesn't have the powerful meaning that PWT does."

Before we left the meeting, I spoke with several people in that group of thirteen. All of them said they practiced PWT in some form. They set aside a specific amount of time—anywhere from five minutes to half an hour—depending on their individual preference.

Call it prayer, call it PWT. I realized they understood one thing. It's a timeout from stress. They make a concerted effort to "save up" all the worries and anxieties that strike throughout the day and deal with them later.

One of the practitioners of PWT told me that he waited until the house was quiet—the time when he used to do his solitary drinking. He said, "It's my time to fret, worry, and get concerned." He couldn't quite get to the place of saying he prayed. He said he had come from a background where prayer held a lot of negative connections. "PWT for me isn't boring or dry or just going through a lot of motions. This is quiet, soft, and totally inward."

I've talked to a few people who have set aside special times for worry. Some call it reflection. One man said, "I just had to have a few minutes every day when I could shut out every sound around me." He's the primary caregiver for his invalid wife. In the mornings when she's resting, he walks through a nearby park for perhaps twenty minutes.

"It's my time to tell God all my problems. When I come back, I feel better."

Whatever we call it, we need time away from the problems, a time when we can reflect on them. Those quiet times are the moments when caregivers can talk to God about their worries, complaints, hurts, as well as their joys and hopes.

"Give all your worries and cares to God, for he cares about what happens to you" (1 Peter 5:7, NLT).

God of peace and comfort, thank you for listening to my complaints, my sadness, and especially my worries, no matter how insignificant they may seem to others. Amen.

Not the Favorite

"I love all of you just the same," her mother said time and again.

"You love Marilyn more than you do me," Loretta insisted.

No matter what evidence she produced, her mother's answer always came back the same way. She insisted she had no favorites, but that she loved them equally, and that she treated all of them the same.

Loretta knew differently, as did Eunice, another sister. Even Marilyn knew she got away with things the others would get punished for.

Rivalries—real or imagined—exist in most families. But what happens when one of the unfavored becomes the caregiver?

Loretta fell into that role because Marilyn couldn't—or wouldn't. Loretta later admitted to me that she had some bitterness for a while over that. "She got all the special treatment when we were kids. I thought it ought to be her turn to pay Mom back."

"I cried a lot when Mom snapped at me," Loretta said. "I tried to remember she was in pain. Her rheumatoid arthritis had crippled her body badly, and no matter how much medication she took, she hurt. I knew that."

She knew, but those stinging words went back more than thirty years. Loretta wondered if she'd yell at Marilyn.

The situation worsened in that family because Loretta's husband had been married before. His first wife died, so Loretta accepted Tom's daughter, Gwen, and then she and Tom had two children of their own. Mom never accepted Gwen.

It came to a head when they discussed Mom's will.

She had listed all the children and grandchildren to receive equal amounts. "Except Gwen," Mom said.

"Gwen is my daughter," Loretta said.

"She is not my granddaughter," she said. "She won't be in my will, and I won't call her my own."

"Then leave my family out. If Gwen is out, our whole family is out."

"I'll do whatever I please with my money," Mom insisted.

"We won't accept it," Loretta said.

They didn't speak of the matter for more than a week until Loretta said, "You know, you treat Gwen the way you treated me. You acknowledged me as your child, but I got about the same treatment as she gets from you."

The mother became enraged and screamed at her daughter. For once, Loretta said nothing until her mother's tirade had ended. "I want to tell you something. Gwen is my child. Accept her or not. If you do not accept her, you do not accept me. But then, I feel as if you have never accepted me."

Her mother started to argue, but Loretta held up her hand. "Just listen."

Her mother stopped and listened.

"You are my mother, and you are my responsibility. I know you don't love me, no matter what you say. I accept that you probably won't change. I'll do the best I can for you because you're my mother."

She went on to insist that her mother treat Gwen with the same kindness she treated the other grandchildren. "If you persist in your favoritism, I will ask you to leave. I will not have Gwen harmed by your cruelty."

"But where will I go?"

"Ask Marilyn." Loretta left the room.

From then on, her mother at least tried to treat Gwen

as well as she treated the others. Her mother is still alive, however, and Gwen is not in the will.

"You know, it's sad growing up not being the favorite," Loretta said. "No matter what I do, I'll never be as wonderful as Marilyn. It still hurts a bit, but I do know I'm giving Mom the best I can. In her own way, she's grateful, but she'll never tell me she's sorry that I'm not her favorite. But I'm all right. I have a supportive family, and they understand and love me."

Loretta made an acute observation, "I think it's like going to the well with an empty bucket. I pump and pump, and there's no water there. I go back with the bucket empty. Sometimes I get a few drops, but mostly I go away empty. That's how it is with Mom. I want her love, but I don't think I'm ever going to get the affection I want. If I keep trying, it's like going back to the dry well."

Like a lot of people, Loretta has to live an imperfect life. She's not going to get everything she wants or feels she needs. "God loves me and so do my kids and my husband. I have a lot of love in my life."

"The steadfast love of the LORD never ceases, his mercies never come to an end; they are new every morning; great is your faithfulness. 'The LORD is my portion,' says my soul, 'therefore I will hope in him' " (Lamentations 3:22–24).

Loving God, I know I'm special to you. Remind me often of that. Amen.

Facing My Anger

"Anger? Yes, I felt anger—a lot of it," Barbara said with an embarrassed smile. "It sounds so irrational now. Mostly, it was directed against Mom. When she got sick, I seethed with fury toward her. She had no right to get sick like that. It was almost as if she had decided to upset our plans."

Barbara and Earl, married twenty-four years before her mother became ill, had dreamed of owning a house in the country, away from the smog and congestion of Davenport, Iowa. "We found the perfect spot—five acres."

Then Barbara's mother became ill, and daily trips were necessary to check on her. Her mother wouldn't move from the house in the west end of Davenport, and Barbara lived in the east end, about a 45-minute drive each way. By moving to their dream spot farther east, it would take two hours to commute each way.

Barbara argued with herself and prayed about the situation for nearly two weeks. In the end, they didn't buy the property—and silent anger blazed at her mother.

Barbara had grown up in the strict Germanic atmosphere that said children did not feel, let alone express, anger toward parents. In every way, they submit to their parents, honor and reverence them. Barbara had done that.

"If you'd live with us," Barbara said, trying to reason with her mother, "that would make things so much better for us."

"My friends live here. This is my home—"

"But you'll have to give it up eventually anyway."

"Then why are you so impatient? You've always been like that, never waiting for anything."

The child had been silenced again, and the anger built.

One day Barbara studied her own reflection in the mirror. She saw the tenseness in her face and felt the tightness in her throat. "You are an angry woman," she said to her reflection.

Sometimes the animosity swelled within her over a simple remark her mother made, such as happened one day when Barbara came to visit. She wore a pleated skirt and a soft, gauzy blouse because she and Earl were going out to dinner with friends.

"You spend too much money for your clothes," her mother said. "You could have gotten that cheaper if you'd have waited for a sale."

Barbara, as usual, said nothing.

"It's not a very good color for you anyway. You need to wear more muted shades. That's a little too bright, if you ask me."

Barbara seethed inside. The next day she set up an appointment with her pastor. The words of anger poured out.

Barbara talked most of the time, but just before she left, her pastor gave her a big tip in dealing with anger toward her mother. "The relationship has changed. It's no longer adult to child. It's adult to adult, especially now that you're caring for her. When you talk to her, remind yourself that you *are* an adult with all the rights and privileges of anyone else your age."

"I've never thought of it that way."

"It's all right to have opinions, to stand up for yourself, and it's all right to disagree. Try it sometime."

A few days later, Barbara's mother criticized her daughter's new haircut.

"I didn't ask you!" Something snapped inside. "I never ask for your opinion! But that doesn't matter."

Once she had opened the door of anger, Barbara couldn't seem to close it again. For several minutes she railed at her mother. "You're still trying to run my life. I'm a grandmother, and you treat me like a little girl!"

"I guess once you're a mother, you just don't know how to stop being one." Her mother broke into convulsive sobbing. "I didn't know, really I didn't! I'm sorry."

Although they made up and assured each other of their love, Barbara left ashamed and depressed. How did I dare speak to her that way? she asked herself. After all, she's my mother. Then she reminded herself that she was also an adult. Her response had been harsh and heated, but at least she had spoken up for herself.

That verbal blowup occurred months ago, and Barbara still doesn't express her anger as openly as she would like. But she's learned to admit to herself that anger is an emotion as natural as joy or contentment.

Two of her friends have encouraged her to express her feelings. They assure her that it's all right to feel whatever she feels.

Slowly, Barbara is progressing. She's learning to disagree with her mother without argumentation. "I just say, 'Mom, this is how I feel.' Then I back off. By not arguing, she's less defensive and more agreeable."

"Be angry but do not sin; do not let the sun go down on your anger" (Ephesians 4:26).

God of peace, I accept anger as a natural emotion, but help me learn to diffuse it by lovingly standing up for myself. Amen.

Tired of Being Healthy

"I'm tired of being healthy all the time," Hannah said. "I'm always taking care of my husband, who had a serious stroke, but I never get any encouragement from him."

I assumed that her resentment was because of his disability and commented to that effect.

Hannah shook her head. "No, he was like that before. It's more than taking me for granted; it's more that I'm his wife—you know, his property—and what I do is what I'm supposed to do."

Hannah is tired—the most common complaint I hear from long-term caregivers. "If there were thirty hours in a day, I'd probably use them up too," she said. "There's never enough time to do everything."

A little appreciation would help her immensely, of course, but she won't get it from her husband. "I have to do everything. If I don't, then I'm a failure, or I'm lazy, or I'm incompetent." She's heard those words from her husband, and she's even begun to repeat them to herself.

"Sometimes I think I'd love the luxury of being too sick to get out of bed. When he would call in his slurred speech, I could say, 'Take care of yourself today. I'm too sick to help.' " Then she laughs self-consciously. "I couldn't do that, but I think about it."

Like many long-term caregivers, Hannah gets caught up in her own abilities and commitments. She has to keep things going, to cope with emergencies and daily care. She has to be a super-coper with an unlimited amount of energy. As her husband fails to function, she's forced to take over, and then she overfunctions. She becomes the epitome of a workaholic.

At the same time, she feels as if she can't ask, "What's

in this for me?" because she focuses on self-denial and bearing his burdens. She puts his interests first, especially as she loses touch with her own.

Some caregivers have developed their own symptoms—obesity and depression are common ones. They often have low self-esteem and feel weighed down by their sense of worthlessness. Instead of being able to focus on all their accomplishments and feeling good about them, caregivers tend to let what's undone claim their focus.

Of course they're tired, but too often they feel they have no right to be sick. Karen told me that she cooked and took care of her sick husband when she had a 104-degree temperature. Yes, she admitted to me, she could have called a daughter or a neighbor, but she didn't. She couldn't be sick. Her job was to be there.

"We try to be more than human and do it all," one woman said. "It's as if we don't have the right to be sick or weak."

One day Hannah tried to explain to her nine-year-old daughter that she had to keep going and be strong and well for Daddy.

"I guess Jesus doesn't love you as much as he does me," the daughter said. Seeing her mother's puzzled expression, the little girl said, "When I'm sick, I hurt, but it's okay. You used to tell me that Jesus loves me all the time, when I'm sick or even when I'm bad."

Hannah grabbed her child, hugged her, and cried a long time. "Thank you, dear," she kept saying.

"Three times I [Paul] appealed to the Lord about this, that it would leave me, but he said to me, 'My grace is sufficient for you, for power is made perfect in weakness' " (2 Corinthians 12:8–9a).

Loving God, whether strong or weak, sick or well, help me know that I'm always loved by you. Amen.

Caring for Caregivers

Too often, caregivers remain the forgotten people. Their loved ones, especially when obviously ill or disabled, easily receive sympathy. Those who stand by the bedside of the seriously ill rarely receive encouragement and sympathy.

After her husband Frank was diagnosed with Alzheimer's disease, Tourette's Syndrome, and Parkinson's, Carole Fulmer needed emotional support and understanding. At that time, he looked normal and still had his long-term memory, so their friends often didn't realize the seriousness of his condition. Carole knew what others didn't and couldn't see. Frank wasn't safe alone. He ordered expensive items advertised on TV and took objects apart but couldn't put them together again. If not carefully watched, he wandered out of the house and became lost.

Worn out from caring for him, Carole needed respite from the twenty-four-hour-a-day ordeal. She asked several people to take care of her husband for short periods of time. They all turned her down. She appealed to the men of her church, where Frank had once been active. "Would you take him for a few hours once a week?" she asked.

Long-term caregivers need helping hands and open hearts. Sometimes it's difficult for them to ask, especially when they've been turned down or ignored previously.

In the more than ten years since her husband's diagnosis, Carole has worked with support groups and followed every other lead she's gotten. "It still hurts when others can't realize how much I need people," she said. "The only ones who really understand are those walking the same path."

One of Carole's worst experiences came from her own church. Because she couldn't leave Frank home alone, she wanted to take him with her to a women's meeting. She had explained this, and one member insisted he couldn't come. When Carole told the leader that she wouldn't come without bringing Frank, she was allowed to bring him.

She's constantly giving care to Frank and reaches out to others, but who reaches out for her? Even worse, she combats insensitive remarks and harsh criticism, such as, "What did you do to make him like that?" The worst time was when one person said, "If you believed in God, this would never have happened."

Like many long-term caregivers, Carole knows the acute loneliness of having no one to lean on, to share with, or to speak of her pain with.

On top of all that, Carole has her own share of physical problems, although she copes well. After one bout of congestive heart failure, she tried several times to get someone to call her every day. "It was just a call to make sure I was all right," she said. One woman agreed to do that. The friend called faithfully for a short time. Then she stopped, leaving Carole feeling even more alone than before.

The saddest story of loneliness came when Frank said he wanted to see the people in their Sunday school class, a class they had attended for years. Believing that the time was limited when he would recognize any of them, she decided on a dinner party. She hired a caterer and arranged for food without consideration of cost. Class members responded and also paid for their own meals, which helped her financially.

At the dinner, none of the people with whom they had associated for years sat at the same table with Frank and

Carole. She asked one couple Frank particularly liked to sit with them. "We don't want to leave our friends," they said. Carole nodded and was overwhelmed with sadness. Who is this party for? she thought. One couple finally came and sat with them. That eased some of the pain, but the damage had been done. Already acutely lonely, Carole felt rejected by the people she had expected to support her.

She knew they weren't purposely being unkind. Maybe that's the worst form of unkindness—when it's unintentional. After dinner, the activities director asked Frank to sing a duet with her of "Amazing Grace."

As she listened, Carole thought of the appropriateness of the hymn. Like many other caregivers, she has learned that survival and growth come down to God's amazing grace. When they look for support and encouragement from their friends, too often it doesn't come. They frequently feel alone. At times there seems little help out there beyond God's amazing grace.

"My help comes from the LORD, who made heaven and earth. . . . The LORD will keep your going out and your coming in from this time on and forevermore" (Psalm 121:2, 8).

Steadfast Lord, when I look for help from others, they often disappoint me. Remind me that you are my unfailing source of help. Amen.

Trapped

"Why do you put up with me?" Jan Johnson's husband asked. "No one else would have stayed with me. I can't do anything for anybody. Why don't you shove me into one of those long-term care places? Who needs me now?"

Hal spoke out of one of his darkest moods. He always seemed tired and depressed after his latest chemotherapy treatment. His harsh, angry words had become a kind of ritual to Jan.

She assured him of her love and her desire to stay with him and to care for him. She also knew that he was probably asking out of fear—fear that she would get rid of him.

Then one pointed question forced Jan into serious self-examination.

"You feel trapped, don't you?" he asked.

Jan started to deny it, and then said, "Sometimes I do, but I love you, and I'll stick with you."

Later that night, unable to sleep, Jan thought of that word—*trapped.* Yes, she did feel trapped. Increasingly, she realized her choices continued to diminish. Although Hal was the sick one, Jan was the prisoner—in her own home.

The outgoing, highly social Jan could no longer do things with friends, or take extended vacations, or spontaneously decide to go hiking for two days in the mountains—the kind of things they had done before Hal's illness.

That triggered other feelings—loneliness, for example. An outgoing person, Jan had loved having friends drop by or chat on the phone. Now the doorbell seldom rang, and friends had stopped calling. No one invited her to social gatherings anymore.

Trapped and *lonely*—those internal words shouted at

her. Tears slid down her cheeks. She felt she had no one to talk to. Who would understand such negative feelings? After all, Hal was dying; she was in good health and alive. Her friends wouldn't understand, even if she tried to explain.

"Alive, lonely, and isolated," Jan said aloud. To make the loneliness more intense, over the past two months Hal had slowly withdrawn. Maybe that was natural, but he had now lost interest in Jan's world and the things they had once shared. He no longer cared about soft sunsets, full moons, and glowing sunrises. They talked less. His dark moods came more often as his condition worsened.

Now caught up in her own dark mood, Jan felt annoyed over the increased workload, and sometimes that annoyance even made her angry. Hal could no longer share the housework. She had to pay the bills and keep tight control over finances. As Jan tossed in bed, she cried again, knowing the situation would only get worse. Hal's dependency would grow. In time, she would have to feed him, bathe him, and lift his weakened body to change the sheets.

Then the most powerful aspect of being trapped filled her mind—Hal's anger trapped her. Often he yelled at the kids if they made noise—just normal, everyday kid noises—or if they spilled milk or dropped a pencil. He screamed at Jan for not having his lunch on time. One time she put smooth peanut butter instead of crunchy in his sandwich. He took one bite and threw it on the floor. "Is it too much to ask just to have good peanut butter around here?"

Hal had been one of those never-sick people until two years ago. He had been the strong one, the fixer, the man who could do just about anything. He was a rising executive in his company. A year from now, he would become a total invalid.

Hal has his own demons to fight, Jan thought, but why take them out on me and on the kids?

Yes, Jan felt trapped. She also knew that leaving him or trying to place him in a nursing facility wasn't the answer. For most of the night, Jan prayed for strength and wisdom. She got out her father's old Bible. He had underlined in yellow the uplifting statements and read them in his dark moments. Jan read and re-read many of them before she finally fell asleep.

The next morning, nothing had changed. Hal yelled for his morning coffee and the newspaper. The kids' usual noises filled the house—another normal day in the Johnson household.

But there was a difference. Jan felt stronger, more able to cope with the day. The sense of being trapped no longer plagued her. She had prayed through the dark hours, and with the morning light came peace. I'm stronger today, she thought. I can't change Hal or the situation, but when I call on God for help, I know I can make it through today. And if I can make it today, I know I'll make all the other days too.

"Weeping may linger for the night, but joy comes with the morning" (Psalm 30:5b).

Heavenly Father, outwardly I sometimes feel trapped, but inwardly I know I'm protected by your loving care. For that, I thank you. Amen.

A Matter of Self-Esteem

"She's so stubborn!" Wanda complained to me about our mother. "She makes up her mind about something, and there's no reasoning with her."

"Yes, she's stubborn," I agreed. "And you're just like her."

She laughed. It was true.

For the last eighteen months of her life, my mother lived with my sister Wanda. Although the youngest of the three sisters, she was the most like Mom in temperament and the most natural one to take her in. Wanda was a widow and lived alone. It worked out well for them. They had many flare-ups, usually a battle of the wills. In the beginning Mom won, but as she grew weaker, she had less force behind her demands.

Mom had had an extremely low sense of self-esteem. I'm surprised I didn't grasp it earlier. Certainly it had been there all her life. I knew enough of her circumstances to understand. Her mother had died when she was quite young, and her father married three times. She felt unloved and unwanted by her stepmothers. I vaguely remember as a boy that the third wife, whom I called grandmother, didn't treat my mother very well.

One way Mom protected herself—and it was probably the way she survived a hard life—was through exerting that strong will. Once Mom made up her mind, she was virtually unbending. Maybe her stubbornness had to do with having to give in so much in her childhood. Maybe it had to do with feeling that to give in meant she was weak and worthless.

I do know that during the last few years of her life I realized how little she valued herself. The real awakening came when she called me one Sunday evening. I lived nearly a thousand miles away. My six siblings all lived in the same city in Iowa.

"Mel hasn't called me all week," she said. Before I could answer, she told me about how terribly he had treated her and that he had borrowed money again the week earlier.

Before she hung up, I could feel anger burning inside me. How dare Mel not call our mother! I dialed his number, and in as few words as possible told him, "You call her right now!"

I don't remember what he said, but I do remember my reaction. As soon as I hung up, I began to laugh. She had done it to me again. I had been the good boy in the family, the fixer, the one who could be depended on and confided in. She expected the other six children to call her every day or to drop by. Because I lived out of state and it would cost money for the calls, that exempted me.

Sometimes it was laughable, such as my call to Mel. At other times it was sad, such as on her seventy-fifth birthday. I sent her a check a week earlier and called the late afternoon of her actual birthday. She started to cry because one son and one daughter hadn't called or come by. "It's my birthday," she said. "They didn't have to stay. Just to come by would be enough."

In a marvelous moment of insight, I realized what was going on. Mom needed to be needed. She needed to know that she was worthwhile and valued. By having her children call, it not only connected her to them; it also gave her a sense of well-being and her world was all right again. It didn't last if they didn't call frequently.

I began to observe my mother's behavior when I visited. She constantly found ways to pull her grown children and grandchildren to her. In subtle ways, she reminded them that even though the family had been poor, she had always taken care of them, and none of us had ever missed a meal. She had grown up during the Great Depression, and there were days she hadn't had food to eat. We heard that frequently while we were growing up.

I've also realized that not only did Mom have a low self-worth issue, so did most of her kids. We learned that at home.

It took many years for me to understand that those who value and love themselves value and love others. That's obvious, but I didn't get it. Further, those who care for themselves try not to degrade, humiliate, or injure others. The more they value themselves, the less they demand from others.

Demand, for me, is the key word. Those who know they are loved don't need to make demands. They receive what they need from the people who love them. Those who don't feel loved and can't love themselves grasp for every possible way to prove they are being loved.

I'll illustrate this with my own case again. I grew up thinking my mother was warm and caring. She hugged me a lot and frequently told me she loved me.

About ten years after Mom's death, my illusive world of childhood shattered when I dealt with a number of my own issues. I vividly recall saying to my wife, "You know, Mom wasn't warm and loving, was she?"

"I always thought she was one of the coldest women I've ever met," my wife said quietly. She never volunteered that information before, because she realized that I needed to believe in that illusion. "*You* were the warm, loving son. You hugged *her* and told her how much you cared."

Had I realized that before she died, I'm not sure what I could have done to make Mom's last days easier. In my case, perhaps my ignorance was a blessing. I know only that Mom lived to the end of her days not feeling worthwhile and always wanting to be loved just for herself.

Perhaps one of the most difficult things caregivers of their parents have to grapple with is that their parents may be needy—not for a place to stay or food to eat. Their neediness is internal. They need to know they're loved and wanted and cared about.

Maybe the best thing we can do for anyone we care for on a long-term basis is to assure them by words and actions that we care. We can't cure their low self-esteem, but we can express the love they need so desperately.

"Be kind to one another, tenderhearted, forgiving one another, as God in Christ has forgiven you" (Ephesians 4:32).

Loving God, you created me out of love and fitted me for love. Enable me to love and to express love to those I care the most for, especially those in my own family. Amen.

Feeling Alone

"I hate living with my daughter," Wayne told me. "Her kids play their music too loud. That dog of theirs thinks my bed is a good place to shed his hair." For several minutes he railed on about the terrible living arrangement.

"Then why do you stay?" I asked.

Wayne blinked rapidly and then lowered his head. In a trembling voice, he said, "I don't want to be alone."

"You mean, you're so afraid of being alone that you'll put up with all the things you hate and complain about?" That was a bit harsh of me, but his words had shocked me.

As we continued to talk, I began to understand. He really felt unloved. He didn't say it in words, but implied that if he wasn't there, he'd never see his daughter. "I turn over my retirement and my Social Security checks. They depend on that money." He looked away then, but I had already seen the moistened eyes. "I don't think she loves me enough to stay involved in my life otherwise."

I knew Wayne's daughter and believed he was mistaken. His feelings may have been wrong, but I didn't feel it was my business to tell him or to ask his daughter to say, "Dad, we want you here." He could ask her himself, but it wasn't so much just the words he wanted spoken; Wayne needed to know—to feel—he was loved.

He told me how he had neglected his family when the kids were growing up. He had put his career first, had rarely attended school events, and seldom went to church with the family. He retired at seventy and had a large financial holding. In his mind, Wayne believed that the prospect of getting his money would bind his daughter to him.

"Maybe there's something more important to bind her."

"You mean love?" He shook his head. "I don't deserve that."

We talked a long time, but nothing was resolved. Even though he could afford to live on his own, he wouldn't. His "rent" (and he made the offer) more than paid his daughter's mortgage bills.

The truth is, Wayne doesn't deserve her love. He wasn't much of a parent during her growing up years. I've heard stories from her and from others of his heavy drinking and his womanizing. Several times he had moved out of the house for a few weeks, but he always came back. No, Wayne doesn't deserve his daughter's love.

Strange as it would have seemed to him, he *had* her love. It wasn't earned; it was just there. "He's my father," was her explanation. She really did love him. One day I asked Wayne if he ever told his daughter that he loved her? "She'd never believe me," he said.

During our several conversations, there were two things I tried to emphasize. One of them is a sign I keep on the door of my office, a saying attributed to Mary Crowley: "People who need love the most deserve it the least." Wayne agreed with that, but it didn't shed any light for him.

We talked about the Jews in the Old Testament. God had chosen them and loved them, and although they failed at every opportunity, God never gave up on them.

He nodded, but couldn't or wouldn't relate it to his own life.

The man exasperated me. His daughter's love and devotion was so obvious. I could see it in her eyes when she looked at him. When she touched him, it was always tenderly.

One day I was sitting with Wayne when his daughter

brought us tea. "It's sad that you don't love this old goat," I said. "He doesn't deserve it anyway. But it is sad."

The shock on her face spoke more than her words. "Of course, I love him," she said and patted his cheek and smiled. "Why else would I put up with him?"

"Maybe you need to listen, Wayne."

He listened, and some of it did sink in. Over the next few months, a little more became obvious to him. I don't know if Wayne will live long enough to realize how deeply his daughter loves him. He's aware of her devotion, but I think he just can't believe he's worth loving.

Somewhere, someway, someday I hope Wayne will get the message. I know his daughter tries to express that love in words now. She's aware, and perhaps has been for a long time, that he can't believe she cares.

"Dad, you're not alone. You'll never be alone as long as I'm alive. Even if something happens to me, you've got a granddaughter who dotes on you."

No, Wayne may never understand how deeply he's loved, and that's sad.

But for now, I hope he can see that he'll never have to be alone. Even if he ends up going to a nursing facility, he'll have the devotion and care he needs.

He won't be alone. He'll always have God at his side. And he'll also have God's human representative—his devoted daughter.

I hope his daughter reflects on that conversation we had. As she realizes how undeserving he feels and how lonely he is, she can ease or even erase those fears.

Sometimes, of course, it works the other way. Many caregivers don't feel loved or deserving of love. They dote on their failures and shortcomings. Or they fail to realize that people who hurt them may speak sharply, sound demanding, and behave impatiently, but it doesn't mean they don't love their caregiver. Because they can't please an aging parent's every wish, too often they feel alone and unloved.

Maybe those relationships won't truly be open until all who are involved can talk more openly about their feelings. Perhaps if those who feel unloved and alone can accept that God loves them and will always love them, that love can pave the way to accept others' caring for them.

[God said] "I have loved you with an everlasting love; therefore I have continued my faithfulness to you" (Jeremiah 31:3b).

Eternal God, at times I feel alone, unwanted, and unloved. Help me understand that you love me, and enable me to accept the love of others. Help me realize that, regardless of my feelings, I'm not alone—ever. Amen.

Resentment

Pauline was the middle child of three sisters. The older was her father's favorite and the younger was mother's. It was one of those things all three grew up knowing. "No one ever said I wasn't loved as much," Pauline said, "but I knew. My sisters knew too."

When mother needed help, Carol, the older sister, had moved from metro-Atlanta to Minneapolis, and they all agreed that their mother would never adjust to those cold winters. The younger sister, Betty, and her new husband (her third) were in a start-up business that demanded most of their time and energy. "We just can't take her," Betty said. "I'd love to if we could. Maybe in a year or two she could move in, but not now."

Mother had to have someone to care for her, and that left only Pauline.

"The situation started on a bad note, and then it got worse," Pauline said. "I could never please her. I wasn't as perfect as Carol or as efficient as Betty. I got tired of hearing how wonderful my sisters were."

The problem began with resentment whose roots went all the way back to early childhood. At times Pauline felt invisible in the family. At the dinner table, Carol sat on her father's right, and Betty was next to her mother. Pauline's place was at the far end with a sister next to her and a sister across from her. "I felt as if my parents didn't know I was there. They talked to my sisters, but rarely to me."

The situation remained that way until all three of the daughters had reached their forties. An unexpected heart attack took their father, and five years later, diabetes and arthritis debilitated their mother so that she could no longer care for herself.

"She wasn't mean or anything like that. I just knew

she would have preferred Betty or even Carol. She got stuck with me. No matter how hard I tried, I knew I would never measure up to either sister."

That little resentment, deeply hidden and never brought into the open before, slowly emerged. It took perhaps a year before it festered like a boil. It came to a head when Mother made an offhand remark about Betty's excellent cooking.

"I know you don't like the way I cook," Pauline said, "but it's the best I can do." She slammed a bowl on the table and spilled pasta all over the fresh tablecloth. "Maybe you'd be better off if you moved in with Betty. She could cook just the way you like it."

Mother stared at her. Her lips trembled, and then she finally said, "She—she doesn't want me."

"That's not true—" But as she started to deny it, Pauline realized it was true. Betty didn't want her mother living with her.

"You're the only one who wants me, the only one who will put up with me." She buried her head in her hands and wept. "You've been good to me. The only one of the three who cares."

Pauline says she felt frozen for several seconds, not able to speak or move. "But, but you're always saying such nice things about them!"

Mother wiped her glasses and stared into her daughter's eyes. "I guess I just needed to assure myself; you know, to fool myself into believing they cared."

Pauline sat down, still shocked at what she had heard. She had grown up in a family that went to church every week and became heavily involved in activities. She often compared her family to that of Isaac and Rebekah. Isaac favored Esau, and Rebekah spoiled Jacob. The problem is, no third child was mentioned. That's why she thought of herself as invisible.

When Pauline's husband came home, he sensed something significant was going on. He hugged his wife and said, "I'll take the kids out to eat. You two need to talk."

Once alone, mother and daughter ate the meal in silence, each woman lost in her private world. Both were afraid to open up the topic again, as they confessed to each other later.

Finally Pauline said matter-of-factly, "You always loved Betty more than you loved me."

"How can you say such a thing?"

"It's true! You did."

Now her mother was amazed. She had never thought about loving one more or less than the other. "I tried—I tried to love all of you the same."

"Maybe if you had tried to love each of us differently, it would have worked," Pauline said. "I'm not Betty or Carol. I just needed a few words of love, of encouragement, of just—just acknowledging I was around. If you'd have just found a place for me in your heart—"

"I tried, really, I tried."

The conversation between mother and daughter didn't end that night. For the next three days, they talked until it became too painful for one of them.

In the end, Mother never quite admitted she preferred Betty, but she did say, "I tried to do right by all of you. I guess I didn't do enough for you. I'm sorry."

Even today, two years since Mother came to live with her, Pauline struggles not to feel inferior to her sisters. They haven't solved all the problems, but they talk.

"You know the best thing that's come out of this?" Pauline said to me. "She hugs me now, and she raises those arthritic arms and invites me to embrace her. She never did that before. Maybe one day all the resentment will die. We're working on it."

"Even if my father and mother abandon me, the Lord will hold me close" (Psalm 27:10, NLT).

God of love and peace, remove my resentment, whether it's over not being loved enough, having to serve, or just feeling stuck here. Remove it so that I can enjoy your peace and thank you for all things. Amen.

Blaming

"Tell me about blame," I asked four long-term caregivers. "Did any of you have any feelings of blaming the person you care for?"

"You mean like blaming them because my life didn't go the way I wanted it to? Or feeling that my life would have been happier without having to care for my mother?"

"You bet! And I still blame my mother!" In rapid-burst sentences, Rose told us her story. She had fallen madly in love with Bill when she was sixteen years old. Bill had already finished high school and had taken his first job in a bank. "We were willing to wait until I graduated, but I loved him. I really did."

The rest of us had already guessed what came next. "My father didn't like it, but it was my mother that absolutely forbade me to me have anything to do with him."

It surprised me to see a woman in her sixties with tear-filled eyes telling me something that happened so long ago.

"They wouldn't let him come to the house. They told me that if I sneaked off and met with him, they'd kick me out." Rose was one of those responsible girls who had never considered disobeying.

"What happened to Bill?" asked one of the group who knew that Rose had married someone else.

"He's a big success in business. Still is. Healthy. Got a ton of grandkids. I haven't seen him in at least twenty years, but I hear about him from mutual friends."

Rose had eventually married a nice man, Harold. Her family had approved because he was a good provider and a faithful churchgoer. They were right about Harold. He was a good man. He worked hard. In fact, during the first years of their marriage, he held down two jobs. Unfortunately, he died of heart attack after nine years of marriage. She had had to bring up three children as a single parent.

"Blame my mother? She ruined my life! I could be happily married to Bill today if it hadn't been for her."

Today, Rose is the sole caregiver for her bedridden mother, who has been diagnosed with colon cancer.

Of the four women who spoke with me, Rose's story was the most dramatic. Ivy's was, in some ways, the saddest. "Until I had to take care of her, my mother was one of those people who could do anything. She managed a house with four children after her divorce, held down a full-time job, and somehow finished her college education.

"She was—and still is—one of the most demanding people I've ever known. I don't mind that she needs to be perfect and to be in control of her own life. Maybe I even admire that. But she's always demanded too much of me.

"For example, one time my husband and I were on vacation, and she got sick. My brother and his wife could have taken care of her. In fact, she was in their home. But Mom called me and asked—no, she demanded—that we disrupt our vacation and come home because she was hurting, and I was the only one who could take care of her properly."

"Did you go?" I asked.

She nodded. "We drove back, and I resented it every mile of the way. The next year when we went on vacation, I purposely didn't leave a number for her to call. I said, 'Oh, I'll phone you when we get there.' I never did. We would have had a wonderful vacation except I knew she's scream at me when I got back. And she did—even worse than I had expected. There was no way to win with her. There still isn't."

One of the group tried to urge her, "Just forgive. You have to forgive."

"Yes, you're right, but maybe not yet," interrupted Ellie, a quiet member of the group. "True, deep forgiveness takes time. It takes a readiness." She told of the anger and blame that she had felt toward her husband. She had been previously married and had a son. The second husband never fully accepted the boy. Ellie blamed her husband for his lack of acceptance; he blamed her for coddling the boy.

"You know, we were both right and both wrong. For at least ten years, my son Robbie was our battleground. I blamed my husband Dan for everything that went wrong in the boy's life. Then one day, I ended up in the hospital with an ulcer. I don't know if it was related, but I do know that for the three days that I lay there, I thought a lot about the family. So much anger and blame had built up toward Dan. I also knew my attitude was wrong."

Ellie said she began to pray for God's help. Forgiveness didn't come. She'd say, "O God, I forgive Dan." Yet within minutes, she'd start seething inside over something he had done in the past.

One day she was reading the Bible and came to the Lord's Prayer. Right in the middle of it, she paused and repeated the petition, "Forgive us our debts, as we also have forgiven our debtors" (Matthew 6:12). Although she had prayed those words before, this time she heard them differently. "Help me want to forgive Dan," she said. "Help me to stop blaming him for everything wrong with Robbie."

That prayer made the difference. She realized that resentment—especially when it's longstanding—isn't easily cast off. It takes time, but eventually forgiveness does come.

Each of the women listened, nodded, and one of them said, "That really is the ultimate answer anyway, isn't it? To forgive."

"It's the only solution," Ellie said. "And if you're not ready to forgive, maybe you could start asking God to make you willing to be ready."

"Forgive us our debts, as we also have forgiven our debtors. . . . For if you forgive others their trespasses, your heavenly Father will also forgive you; but if you do not forgive others, neither will your Father forgive your trespasses" (Matthew 6:12, 14–15).

God of grace, thank you for not blaming me for failures. Instead, you have forgiven me. Help me do the same for others. Amen.

Feeling Guilty

Maxine had smoked for more than twenty years. It devastated her when her mother, a nonsmoker, was diagnosed with lung cancer. "I caused it," Maxine said. When doctors and friends tried to talk her out of her feelings, she listened, nodded, and realized that it wouldn't do any good to argue. The guilt didn't go away.

A few months ago when she and I talked at length, she said, "Guilt is my best friend, and I can always count on her presence. I go to buy groceries, and she constantly chatters that I need to be back at the house taking care of Mom. I put off a dental appointment for nearly three months until my brother came to visit. Yep, she's with me all the time."

The worst thing anyone said to Maxine was, "Guilt is a totally unproductive emotion." Quite rightly, the remark made her angry, as if she didn't know better.

Maxine stared in shock and then asked, "And how do I get rid of it?"

"Pray," the friend said. He told her how to pray and quoted a number of verses, but his advice didn't help.

"In fact, I think I felt worse afterward," she said. "If I understood what he was trying to say, it was that guilt was bad enough, but if I didn't let it go, I was a worse sinner for holding on." She snorted. "As if I could release it!"

Years ago, I read that guilt is anger we think we don't have the right to feel. Maybe that's true, although I think it's more. Guilt, at least for me, is the feeling of having done too little or not done enough.

Whatever the nature of guilt, all of us who feel it know one thing—it's not a good feeling. We'll do a lot of things to get rid of it. Some take pills or alcohol to mask it. But it's still there.

Guilt is one emotion I sense with many long-term caregivers. They're constantly looking at their shortcomings or at what they might have done better. No matter how hard or long they work, something gets left undone. Or like Maxine, they may feel guilty over their loved one's illness. "If I had watched her more closely." "If only I had demanded that Dad quit smoking (or drinking or overeating) years ago when I knew it could kill him."

Maxine quit smoking—too late to benefit her mother. Her mother lived in an environment with many smokers around, so it probably meant that Maxine wasn't the single cause. That still didn't help.

One day when she was the most guilt-laden, she told me how she was feeling. I, in turn, shared with her an experience of mine. Years ago, I had a difficult problem and a situation where I had failed and lived with a heavy burden of guilt.

I shared it with a minister, Dr. Robert Ramey. "You're too hard on yourself," he said, as if I didn't know that. But the next words changed my life. "You're a compassionate person, so why don't you offer yourself a little of that compassion?"

"If I knew how, I'd do it," I said.

"If Cec was your friend, would you feel compassionate toward him? forgive him? assure him it was all right?" Of course, I would. "Then pray for him, as if he were a third party. Ask God's mercy and forgiveness as you would for any friend."

I followed Dr. Ramey's advice and forgave myself. It took a while, and it felt awkward, but I did it.

After I shared this with Maxine, her eyes lit up. "You know, that makes sense. I can do that. I can step back and look at myself as if I were somebody else." Like me, it took Maxine a long time, but eventually she was able to lay aside the guilt.

"And Jesus said, 'Neither do I condemn you. Go your way, and from now on do not sin again' " (John 8:11b).

Forgiving God, I often forgive others more easily than I forgive myself. Help me to forgive me—just the way you forgive me. Amen.

Stressed Out

"I'm tired all the time," Kathryn said. "It doesn't seem to matter how many hours I sleep. When I wake up, I'm still tired. I try to rest more, but my mind won't relax."

That's stress—a word we hear often in our world today. Although stress is a part of living in the modern world, those who provide long-term care sometimes feel as if stress is synonymous with caregiving.

The worst thing anyone can say as a way to help is, "Relax! Just push away the stress."

"Relax? Meditate? Pray? Get alone?" one woman asked. "If I could find time to do any of those things I wouldn't feel so stressed. I'm on the go around the clock. Don't you get it? That's why I'm stressed."

Physically, stress works like this. Whenever we face something that produces fear or anger, and we can't respond with the "fight-or-flight" response, we internalize the pressure. Our sympathetic nervous system responds immediately with increased blood pressure, our heart beats faster, and our respiratory rate soars. Sometimes we sweat. We also know that stress decreases our body's own cancer-fighting chemicals. Our immune system fights bacteria and infection, fungi, cancer, and other invasions that try to destroy our health. Stress makes us more susceptible to such invasions.

"I'm not tense," one caregiver said to me. For her a tense body meant stress. What she didn't realize is that stress comes in a variety of ways. Sometimes it means people can't concentrate or become forgetful. Some feel heart palpitations. Others can't sleep, or they sleep too much.

Stress can show in headaches or tightness of the shoulders. Commonly people complain of backaches, which we know is another form of tension. Obsessive worrying, panic, shakiness, irritability—all of them fit into the category of stress.

When I was a pastor, I used to follow up the bereaved in our congregation. Over the years, I realized how often the grief-stricken became ill soon after the death of a loved one. When my father died, my mother came down with a virulent cold within three days, which I'm sure was stress related.

We're also learning that chronic stress can—and does—eventually lead to chronic illness. We have even diagnosed several diseases as stress related or at least aggravated by stress.

So what can Kathryn do about her stress? She's learned several relaxation techniques, and they help some.

"I finally figured out why I'm under such stress," she said. "For me, it's the inability to accept things as they are. I don't like Mom being sick. I don't like it that she's become incontinent or that I have to wash her bed linens every day. I don't like having to check on her six or eight times a day."

Kathryn also realized that once she accepted her powerlessness—and for her that meant her lack of control over the factors of her life—she was able to cut down the stress. "I think of stress as fighting God. I'm not going to change things. I can pray, and perhaps that will make a difference. But God's still the one with the master plan. If I try to thwart that plan, I fight God."

For Kathryn, releasing stress meant surrendering her will to God. Many times she's had to forgive herself. "The worst times are when I think, life isn't supposed to be this way. When I think what a good person Mom has always been or that other people deserve such terrible sickness, then I'm in trouble. But when I say, 'Okay, God, I'm in your hands. I give up,' God's peace slowly seeps into my life."

"Do not worry about anything, but in everything by prayer and supplication with thanksgiving let your requests be made known to God. And the peace of God, which surpasses all understanding, will guard your hearts and your minds in Christ Jesus" (Philippians 4:6–7).

God of peace, free me from unhealthy stress. Teach me to rely on you and to surrender control to you. Amen.

Pampering Myself

"What's your mischievous pleasure?"

What a strange question that may sound like for long-term caregivers! Aren't we the people who need encouragement just to cope with our task twenty-four hours a day? Who has time for pleasure, especially ones called mischievous?

"The word *mischievous* sounds like fun," my friend Carla said. "Who has time for fun these days?" She spoke as one who knows. Her mother is a semi-invalid, her father is in a nursing facility, and she still has two children living at home.

I had caught her as she tried to dart out of worship after the early service at our church. Once active in our Sunday school class and women's circles, on most Sundays Carla rushed late into the early service. Sometimes she went out the side door during the final hymn.

"You mean, if you're two minutes late today, your family will go into chaos?" I asked.

She shook her head and laughed. "I guess I'm so used to hurrying that I feel as if I'm always on a treadmill."

"Maybe it's time to pamper yourself."

Before Carla could again call me crazy, I said, "You know I work hard all week. On Friday afternoon I turn off my computer and rarely turn it on to do any work until Monday morning." Her arched eyebrow asked why I was telling her.

"Here's what I discovered. For the first seven or eight years of being a full-time writer, I wrote six days and again a couple of hours after church. The pressure to make a living was intense.

"Then it dawned on me one day that I needed to relax,

to give in, and to enjoy my life. I learned that when I gave in and did something to distract myself, it did wonders for me. It gave me a chance to catch my breath and to re-focus."

I hugged her and said, "You might want to think about that."

Carla stared at me. "I hear what you're saying, and I know you're right—"

I held up my hand. "Don't say *but*. When you do, you refute everything that's been said."

She laughed, gave me another hug, and rushed off.

Perhaps a month later, I saw Carla at a restaurant with her husband. When I hugged her, she whispered, "This is mischievous pampering. And, hey, it works."

It's difficult for some people to pamper themselves, but maybe they need it. They need to think about it and decide what's fun for them. If they'll allow themselves to push their stresses away for a few hours, they'll feel recharged afterward.

I've heard of all kinds of mischievous pamperings—an hour-long soak in a hot tub, getting a facial and a man-icure, watching a daytime drama each afternoon.

One woman waits until her husband gets home from work and says, "Mom's all yours now." For at least forty-five minutes, she works in the backyard with her flowers. She loves to get down on her hands and knees to dig out the weeds one at a time. When she's away from the house and in the backyard, she's lost in the greenery around her. Even in winter, she finds things to do out there to pamper herself.

A friend used to hire a neighbor to come over for an hour five afternoons a week. She drove to a nature pre-serve and walked. She wrote Bible verses on 3 × 5 cards and read them as she walked.

What we do isn't important. The fact that we carve out a regular diversion does matter. It gives us perspective. It's a chance to do something for ourselves.

Too many caregivers focus on the other person so intently, they neglect themselves. It's not unusual for such caregivers to have serious health problems, especially after the loved one goes into a nursing facility or dies. It's almost as if they have held their own physical needs in abeyance. When the parent or the mate no longer demands full-time care, then it's time for them to get sick. Sadly, they could have avoided much of their own physical pain had they learned to pamper themselves along the way.

When you finish reading this meditation, put the book down, go into the bathroom, and close the door. Ask yourself this question: "What's my mischievous pleasure?" Listen to your heart. Ask God's help. What would make you feel temporarily better, inspire you, or ease your troubled heart?

Answer yourself. Then do it. Fulfill your mischievous pleasure.

"Answer me when I call, O God of my right! You gave me room when I was in distress. Be gracious to me, and hear my prayer" (Psalm 4:1).

Generous God, you care about me and my life. I believe that when I enjoy my life, you take pleasure in that. Help me free myself to enjoy moments of mischievous pleasure. Amen.

If Only . . .

"If only I had been there when she fell. She lay on the floor in pain for two hours."

"If only I had been there when Daddy had his stroke."

"If only I had realized how sick she was and had gotten her to the doctor sooner."

The if-only syndrome hits a lot of long-term caregivers.

Tammy probably had the worst case of if-onlys that I considered. Her life is now stable with her second husband (after one divorce and two live-ins). She has been involved in AA meetings for two years, and at age forty-four she has had a spiritual conversion. Finally, she experiences the kind of relationship with God that her mother had always wanted her to have.

Tammy and her family worshiped at the same church for more than three years. Then came Mom's first myocardial infarction. With only mild damage, she lived an almost normal life for the next couple of years. Further complications physically limited her lifestyle and made her more dependent on her daughter.

"If only I had lived right all those years," Tammy said often. "If only I hadn't been such a wild person." She spoke of the worry and strain on her mother and added, "If only I had listened to her advice and lived the way she taught me."

Every time her mother's condition worsened, Tammy felt plagued by guilt and a sense of failure.

Her brother, Lance, tried to console her. "Mom is so proud of you for turning your life around." He spoke of their mother's love and acceptance, but got nowhere. He tried reason, but Tammy's problem defied logical analysis.

"I'm responsible. It's my fault. If only I had—"

"Stop!" Lance said. For almost an hour, Tammy had backed into her if-only corner, no matter what he said. "You need to change your way of thinking."

"Oh, of course. Just tell me how."

"Okay, do you believe Jesus Christ has control over your life? over Mom's life? Or do you think your stubborn will overrides all that?"

"He's all powerful—"

"But not powerful enough, right? Because of the way *you* behaved in the past, no matter what God or Mom or anyone else wanted, your evil ways were stronger."

"Okay, I get it. It makes sense," she said,

Yet both knew she still had a lot of emotional upheaval to go through. As the firstborn in the family, Tammy accepted responsibility for Lance and Ruth (who lived in another state). In childhood, when anything went wrong, she felt she had failed. Her parents never said that, but it was the emotional message she received.

"Maybe your problem is that you need to forgive yourself," said Lance.

"Maybe you're right. I've prayed and prayed about that, but nothing seems to change."

"Have you forgiven yourself for not being perfect?"

Lance's words hit her powerfully, and she didn't answer. She had never thought about being perfect, although she knew he was right when he spoke. If she were truly perfect, she wouldn't have those regrets.

Lance grabbed Tammy's hand and took her into their mother's room. "Mom, she thinks she's the cause of your heart problems. She thinks that if she had lived better or become a believer sooner or done things differently, you wouldn't be sick today."

Their mother listened as her two children talked about

guilt, perfection, and responsibility. That mother was astute enough to say, "I don't know if you had anything to do with it. I've never blamed you, and I don't know if my worry over you affected my heart. I do know you're the best daughter I could ever hope to have."

She held out her arms and embraced Tammy.

"I'm in God's hands now," her mother said and smiled. "And you know what? I've been there a long, long time."

That experience didn't solve everything for Tammy, but it did ease things for her. When she finds herself thinking "If only," she reminds herself, "God is in control. I don't have to be responsible for everything that happens."

"I am God, and also henceforth I am He; there is no one who can deliver from my hand; I work and who can hinder it?" (Isaiah 43:13).

Understanding God, forgive me for thinking everything depends on me. When I admit it all depends on you, my life goes much more smoothly. Amen.

PART FIVE

Caring until the End

A Matter of Time

A few months before my father died, I felt the urgency to visit him. He and my mother were still living in their house, but two of my sisters and a sister-in-law spent a lot of time with them and phoned them every day.

Although I couldn't have put it into words, I sensed that I needed to say things to my father—the things I had been wanting to tell him most of my life. I wanted to talk about my pain, my sense of abandonment, and my not feeling loved by him. As the fifth of seven children, I always felt I was the most respected but the least loved. Quite early, it became apparent to my older siblings and my parents that I would turn out to be the most self-reliant.

All of us knew it was only a question of time before Dad died. The effects of alcohol, smoking, and not taking care of himself had finally worn Dad down.

I didn't expect Dad to change. When I visited, he behaved exactly as I had anticipated. I had flown a thousand miles to be with him for three days, but it wasn't until the last night that I finally got to be alone with him. "I have several things I need to say," I told him.

He sat down in his rocking chair across the room and listened while I rolled out all the pain. Dad, who was an extremely quiet person anyway, listened but said nothing.

I finished by saying, "I've only wanted one thing from you. I wanted your love. I've never felt I ever had it."

When I finished he nodded slowly. "Hmm, well," he said. He left the room.

I didn't see him again until just before I left the next day. That was also the last time I ever saw him alive. About two months later, Dad died of a stroke.

I never heard the words from him I wanted to hear. I

can make excuses for my father. He didn't know how to express himself or have any sense of using the language of love. Regardless, the words I yearned to hear never came.

At least I did express how I felt. I knew the end was coming for him. Aside from the commonsense observations, intuitively I knew it was the last time we would ever talk. That feeling was correct.

Mine is a story without an ending. I know of others who have found the right ending for theirs. They have talked—both parent and child. They have reconciled the differences and dissolved the pain. It can happen. Even if it doesn't, we can try to bridge the differences.

The urgency of time is one factor that makes such happenings possible. The parent becomes aware that the end is closer. The child knows it's a matter of waiting because the end seems so obvious.

What better time to come together, to bring all things into the open! The length of years doesn't really mean much. I thought of the story of Jacob, when his son Joseph presented him before the Pharaoh of Egypt. When the ruler asked Jacob's age, he said, "The years of my earthly sojourn are one hundred thirty; few and hard have been the years of my life" (Genesis 47:9b).

Jacob lived long enough to bless each of his sons. We have only a highly condensed version of the story. I hope it's not reading too much into what isn't written, but I like thinking that a lot of confessing and forgiving went on. The older brothers certainly must have told Jacob that, out of jealousy, they had sold Joseph as a slave and then lied to protect themselves from blame. We have no way of knowing what happened, but we do know that as the old man prepared to die, all twelve sons were there. They talked, and the father blessed them. That sounds like a wonderful closure.

In this story, Joseph was alive, so his brothers had to explain their reason for selling him. That's when I think the reconciliation came. For others, it may happen when all parties know the end is coming.

Even if no changes occur—as in my case—we can still reach out. Just the act of reaching out toward my dad and telling him how I felt brought an inner calmness. Others speak of similar experiences. Doing what we can and knowing we have tried may not be a resolution, but it can give us peace.

"But I trust in you, O LORD; I say, 'You are my God.' My times are in your hand" (Psalm 31:14–15a).

"Do not cast me off in the time of old age; do not forsake me when my strength is spent" (Psalm 71:9).

Steadfast God, help me, and remind me that I'm not responsible for anyone else's life, emotions, or feelings. Yet while there is still time, help me find peace and understanding with those I love. Amen.

Second Childhood

"I'm overwhelmed, and I feel pulled in every direction," said Susan. "Everybody wants a piece of me—my mom, my kids, my husband. Some days I want to drop out of the human race. I want to lock myself in a room and cry or scream."

For Susan, her predicament was extremely hard because her mother had been diagnosed with Alzheimer's disease. Moreover, Susan's friends have difficulty understanding her concern. "Why, she looks fine. I've never seen her looking more healthy."

They couldn't seem to take in that her mind and memory were slowly disappearing. One neighbor laughingly said, "Oh, it's just a second childhood. A lot of older people go through it."

It's never easy to care for a parent, no matter what the diagnosis. But when the parent is only an outward shell, it hurts deeply.

Susan wondered how her friends could talk so callously about it. When she complained about the amount of work, a family friend asked, "How much extra work can it be?" Then she quoted the old saying, "One mother takes care of ten children, but ten children can't take care of one mother."

Those words riled Susan. "How can you compare them? Raising children and caring for your parent are different—totally different."

Before her friend could argue, Susan said, "Think about it. I watch my children grow. From day to day, I see the difference. They're getting taller, their weight increases, and they're learning to be more independent. Each day I watch Mom decline. Things she could do a month ago now confuse her. She used to know how to cook simple breakfasts. Now she stares at the stove, not sure how to turn it on. One day I picked a lovely black-eyed Susan from my garden. It was her favorite flower— that's why I'm named Susan. You know what she did? She put it in her mouth and tried to eat it. If caring for her is anything like caring for a child, then it's caring backward!"

"Of course, there are similarities," Susan admitted. "When my kids were too small to do things for themselves, I had to watch them all the time. I couldn't allow them to cross the street or walk to the playground alone. That's how it is with Mama. I have to watch her all the time. And it gets harder every day."

Susan doesn't have a lot of outside support. Her friends are beginning to notice the strange behavior. Her mother doesn't recognize her friends. When asked, she says, "Of course I know who you are. Do you think I'm stupid?" She plays little games to avoid detection, but Susan knows they won't last long.

Susan cries a lot—sometimes for herself and sometimes for her loss. Often it's for her mother. "Some days I tell God I can't take it any longer. That's how I feel, but I also know I can keep going. I have to keep on."

Susan learned, as many do, that we read the inner thoughts of those in turmoil. We may not understand their peculiar circumstances, but we empathize with them in their pain. It's one way to combat the ongoing grief of seeing a loved one's life diminish.

Susan's mother's condition is more than a second childhood. It's a serious loss and a movement toward total loss of the person we love.

"As for me, I am poor and needy, but the Lord takes thought for me. You are my help and my deliverer; do not delay, O my God" (Psalm 40:17).

God of comfort, thank you for words such as we find in the Bible. Thank you for those biblical writers who coura- geously wrote in the midst of their suffering. Now as I read those words, they provide comfort in my pain. Amen.

Life Patterns

"How long do you expect her to live?" we asked the doctor.

"You probably know that better than I do," she said. "It could be a day or two months."

Does that sound like a doctor who doesn't know her business? Actually, it's the wisdom of one who probably knows her business well.

After we transferred Edith to the hospice section of the nursing facility, someone gave us a book whose title I don't remember. The most significant thing I read in it was a statement that most people die the way they live. Those who do things slowly and methodically tend to die the same way. Edith was like that. "No one ever pushes Edith to hurry," her brother once said. "She has her pace, and she sticks with it."

That's when I knew Edith would be one of those who linger. Even though one nurse was sure that it would be any time and a hospice worker echoed the same words, Shirley and I knew it wouldn't happen soon.

She stayed in the nursing facility from early February until her death in mid-December. She moved slowly. That was her way—the pattern she had set during her life.

We all have rhythms and patterns in life. I like to think we sing the same type of songs all our lives. We all know of people who get diagnosed one week and leave this life the next. "He just gave up on life," people often say.

That may be true. But I'd like to think that the person followed a normal pattern. Those who do things quickly all through life tend to end things just as quickly. If given any choice in their treatment, they don't choose to linger.

As we focus on those we love and as we offer them the best care we can, we also need to honor their life patterns. How did they do things when they were healthy? If they were brusque or sweet, they'll probably be the same after sickness comes.

Years ago, someone said, "People change. But they don't change much." Most caregivers know that. If they're in tune with the sick person, they know that person will behave according to what is normal for him or her.

At the nursing facility, Edith's roommate was stubborn and difficult. Shirley made a comment to her daughter, "I suppose as she gets sicker, she gets that way."

The daughter shook her head. "Mom has always been that way. She may be a little worse now, but, no, she's always been hard to get along with."

Accepting that reality makes it easier for caregivers. I think of one woman who agreed to let her mother-in-law live with them. They had never been able to get along well. She complained, "I assumed that because she was sick and had to depend on me to do things for her she'd be different. Ha! Was I in for a shock."

The same woman also said, "It took me a while, but once I accepted that she was the same woman I had known for over twenty years, we got along. I ignored the things about her I didn't like—the same way I've done all through my married life. It worked."

When we respect others' life patterns instead of trying to change them, we make it easier for them. We also make it easier for ourselves. The fighting can stop, and we can focus on caring for them just as they are.

"Let love be genuine; hate what is evil, hold fast to what is good; love one another with mutual affection; outdo one another in showing honor" (Romans 12:9–10).

Reassuring God, you love and accept me as I am. Help me do the same for others. Amen.

The Last Chance

"I had turned fifty-one the week before I got the news," Annette said. "My sister, Jenny, two years younger, was in the advanced stages of leukemia. Her doctors didn't offer much hope. Her kidneys had failed, and she had to go twice weekly for dialysis."

Jenny's husband had divorced her shortly after the original diagnosis. Jenny's only daughter had died in an accident during her teens.

"I was the only one left to care for her."

For a few days, Annette struggled over the situation. She thought of the old rivalry between them. "She was prettier than me. During high school she stole my boyfriends." The heart of the rivalry, however, went back to early childhood when they competed for the attention of a father who was rarely home because he traveled five days a week. Although their mother came home each night, her career took most of her energy. By nature, she wasn't as nurturing as their father. "Our parents seemed to have so little time for us," Annette said, "that when they were around, we fought for their attention. I guess we were starved for affection and didn't have the maturity to share."

A week before Jenny moved in, Annette asked four members of her Sunday school class to come to her house. She asked them to offer a special prayer just for her and Jenny. "We'll be at each other's throats unless God intervenes," she said. Although she knew Jenny wouldn't be physically strong enough to argue, the rivalries and pain would still be there between them.

"What do you want us to pray about?" asked Florence.

"That we'll make these last days a time of healing for both of us."

The four women counseled her and prayed for her. Before they left, each woman agreed to continue praying for the two sisters every day.

Jenny lived eight months with her sister. They had ups and downs, but it did become a time of healing. It was the last chance for the sisters to finish the "business of life," as Jenny put it. They learned to talk, and more important, both learned to forgive.

"It really surprised me how much anger Jenny had stored against me. She said I was always the perfect daughter, the one who couldn't do anything wrong. I never knew she felt inferior to me."

Jenny said she stole her sister's boyfriends because it was the only way she had a chance at winning. They discussed their rivalry over their parents' affection and everything else that kept them apart. Now was their time to bring about healing.

"We touched a lot in those last days," Annette said. "I don't remember ever having hugged my sister before. I'm sure I did, but I couldn't remember."

Sometimes the two women sat and held hands as they talked quietly. Annette would read each afternoon from the Bible. "I sat close enough so that some part of our bodies touched. That seemed important to both of us. It was as if we had found each other at last, and we didn't want to be separated."

The two sisters never understood all the ties that bound them together—some real, some mysterious or unexplainable—but they were bound together. Those months became their last chance to live and love, not only as physical sisters, but also as spiritual sisters.

During those last days, Annette felt an overwhelming flow of love for Jenny. "I knew then that I loved her as much as I loved myself."

Annette started to say just those words, but Jenny spoke first. In a voice so weak Annette had to lean close to hear her, Jenny said, "We both know what love means now, don't we? We've done it."

"Yes, we have," Annette said and embraced her frail sister.

It took a long time after the funeral before Annette could talk about her sister, but one time she shared with her Sunday school class. "It was our last chance to wrap it all up, to get rid of the pain and animosity between us. And we did. We made the best of our last chance."

" 'Teacher, which commandment in the law is the greatest?' [Jesus] said to him, 'You shall love the Lord your God with all your heart, and with all your soul, and with all your mind.' This is the greatest and first commandment. And a second is like it: 'You shall love your neighbor as yourself.' On these two commandments hang all the law and the prophets" (Matthew 22:36–40).

Loving God of all eternity, in this long-term caring situation, help me to make the best of things. It may well be my last chance to love and to open myself fully to my loved one. Grant both of us the ability to do that. Amen.

Healing and Hope

"You have no right to try to take away my hope," Stella Burns said to her pastor. He was trying to be helpful. Stella's sister had fought leukemia for four years. Twice she had gone into short periods of remission. Now everything pointed to the end.

Stella had asked her pastor for prayer for her sister. She pointed out the words in James 5 that say to call the elders of the church. "I want you to bring oil and at least one elder, lay hands on my sister, and pray for her."

I wish the pastor had complied without trying to straighten out her theology. He offered her a rational argument about her sister being far too close to death. He didn't believe it would do any good.

I liked Stella's reply: *"You have no right to take away my hope."*

When people are in long-term caregiving situations, they need hope—even the slimmest chance—that something wonderful will happen. God can perform miracles. It might happen. The Bible, especially the New Testament, is filled with examples of healing of a man born blind, a man crippled thirty-eight years, and even a few instances of being raised to life after being pronounced dead.

What's wrong with asking for a miracle? with praying for healing? with looking for divine intervention? Who has the right to say to another person, "God doesn't do that anymore" or "God won't do that"?

Long-term caregiving isn't an easy task of living for people who live in such a situation of sickness every single day of the year, with no time off. The responsibility is always there. Because the Bible records healing experiences, we have an example of intervention. God exhorts us to ask, to bring our needs to the divine one.

We're all different, and some believe strongly in what we call divine healing. For those who do, friends and supporters need to honor that belief, to encourage them in any way they want encouragement. If the pastor had prayed for Stella's sister and there had been a miracle of healing, there would have been great rejoicing.

It wasn't the pastor's responsibility to bring about results. He was there to honor the request of a sad, grieving woman. The request wasn't so much a deep belief in healing as it was a final effort for Stella.

Stella found another pastor who came with several elders, rubbed oil on the sister's forehead, and they prayed. The sister did not improve, although Stella said, "How do we know unless we ask God to do something?"

That request for prayer was an important step for Stella in her caregiving. She was crying to God for help, but she was doing more. In her own way, she was moving toward acceptance of death.

She was talking about hope, but a lot more. "It was like a message from God that said, 'I've heard you, but my plan will proceed.'"

She didn't think of God as cruel or uncaring. Her faith in a loving, caring God enabled her to say, "This is the will of God, and I accept it." Stella said that from then on until her sister's death, she felt a deep peace.

"I had done my best. Now my sister was in God's hands." She paused, nodded in contemplation, and then added, "But then, she's always been in God's hands, hasn't she?"

"When this perishable body puts on imperishability, and this mortal body puts on immortality, then the saying that is written will be fulfilled: 'Death has been swallowed up in victory.' 'Where, O death, is your victory? Where, O death, is your sting?' . . . But thanks be to God, who gives us the victory through our Lord Jesus Christ" (1 Corinthians 15:54–55, 57).

Caring God, remind me that no matter what measures I take for my loved one, I still know my loved one is in your hands. Amen.

The Right Time

Maybe we could call it the final act of love for those we care about. In some ways, it's the hardest. It's that moment when we help our loved ones surrender to the end of life. Being Christian or having a strong religious faith helps them. But no matter what, they have to let go.

Sometimes our loved ones can do it unaided. For example, Janie Barton was dying from cancer, but she kept holding on until her youngest child, Tina, got married. The family brought Janie to the wedding in a wheelchair, and she sat through it all.

During the reception, she called over Woody McKay, the pastor. "I want to say good-bye to you now," she said. Both knew exactly what she meant.

The next day, Janie died. She had decided when it was time.

Not everyone is able to make that choice unaided. Some hang on simply because they don't have the assurance that it's all right to die. Moreover, one of the hardest tasks—and one of the most demanding acts of love—is for caregivers to ask, "Are you ready?"

Over a thirty-year period, I've asked that question of five people. It was never an easy question to ask. I'll never forget the first person I asked. His name was Tommy Thompson. His wife and two daughters had stayed with him through a prolonged battle with cancer. They finally brought him to the hospital to die.

"It will be any time now," the doctor said, "maybe within hours."

To everyone's surprise, Tommy didn't die. For three days he lay in the hospital. I spoke with the family; I prayed with them; I prayed for and with Tommy. Nothing changed.

On my way to the hospital the third evening, quite suddenly I knew why Tommy lingered. The family hadn't released him. He felt as if he had to keep holding on for them.

Yes, it does happen. Despite medical evidence that says the person can't possibly live, they hold on until they're ready.

After consulting the family, I said, "Tommy, the family is ready to release you. They love you, but they will get by without you." I waited until I was certain he had absorbed that before I asked, "Are you ready, Tommy? Ready to meet God?"

He nodded, and we prayed together.

One by one, Tommy's wife and children came in to see him, hug him, and express their love. "Tell him good-bye in your own way," I had said, "but let him know that it's all right."

Twenty minutes after his wife kissed him and left, Tommy died. It was time.

My last experience occurred in August 1998 when I asked Edith if she was ready. "They still need me," she said.

I never figured out what that meant, and it wasn't important for me to know. Her words told me that she wasn't ready to die, even though cancer had crept all through her body. When she was ready, she asked me to pray for her.

Nearly four months later, Edith said she was ready. Her face radiated joy, and she said, "Carl [her husband] is waiting for me now."

I had completed the final act of love. I wept so hard, I could hardly finish praying. I left almost immediately and walked around outside for maybe half an hour. Something strange had happened to me. In offering Edith that final act of love, I realized that I, too, was letting go. Shirley and I had talked of her leaving us. For ten months we had known it was inevitable. Yet in that moment of relinquishment on my part, the pain and grief swelled up.

It would soon be over. Edith was ready to go. She died two days later. It was the right time.

"Our soul waits for the LORD; he is our help and shield" (Psalm 33:20).

God of time and God beyond time, help me to release those I love into your capable and caring hands. Amen.

Making the Move

"I did it all wrong, and if you want the textbook approach on how not to do it, I'm the expert," Ginny Ray said. After Ginny's mother died, it became apparent to Ginny that her father couldn't live alone. It wasn't only his health problems. He constantly forgot to take his medicine, no matter how well laid out it was. He wouldn't get out of bed and exercise the way the doctor wanted him to.

"I prepared my kids, and they took it fine," she said. "They liked Gramps, who was quiet and, at times, funny." Over the next three years, Gramps became part of the family, but his health slowly declined.

"When he became incontinent and unable to walk, I knew it was time to send him to a nursing care facility," she said.

Ginny knew he would resist going, but she went ahead, made arrangements, and then told Gramps. Before he could object, she said, "It really isn't bad there."

"If it's not so bad, you go there! I ain't going."

"You have no choice," she said. "It's all set."

"Like I have no rights? I have no say-so in this? Now that I'm trouble, you just want to pitch me out?"

The recriminations and accusations flew between them. Issues that spanned nearly forty years came out. "You're as mean as ever! You never really loved me anyway," Ginny screamed.

"You were always the hardheaded kid in the family. You haven't changed!"

They finally calmed down. Ginny apologized, and then Gramps apologized. When she informed her siblings, another battle ensued because she hadn't consulted them. They knew Gramps was getting worse, but Ginny hadn't kept them informed on how bad he was. "I didn't want to add any stress on you. I thought it would be easier if I went ahead."

As Ginny talked to three of us about institutional long-term care, she said, "The first mistake I made was that I never thought about Gramps' feelings." Only later did she realize Gramps was scared. His daughter and her family had taken good care of him.

Years earlier, one of his friends had gone to a different facility. Whenever Gramps visited, he had to listen to a list of complaints and terrible inconveniences. Even though Gramps admitted to himself that his friend had always been a complainer, whenever Gramps visited, he felt uncomfortable in the facility. I won't ever go to be in an awful place like this, he vowed to himself.

"Don't I have any choice?" was the question that finally got through to Ginny.

She almost snapped back, "No! You don't!" Instead she heard something in his voice. She didn't recognize it as fear, but it meant something far deeper than the question he asked.

"Gramps, I'm sorry. We love you, and you know that. We'd keep you with us if we could."

Just then, Ginny's six-year-old daughter came into the room. "I don't want you to go. I'll help Mommy more if you stay. I'll change your smelly bed every day for you and help with the washing." She hugged him. "Don't go. Stay here with us."

Gramps stared into her eyes, and he said quietly, "No, I have to move. It's best for everyone." (He later said that was when he realized the hardship his staying placed on his daughter and family.)

The family moved him three days later. They faithfully

visit as much as they can. Gramps sleeps most of the time now and sometimes doesn't wake up. His cancer is systemic, and they all know it's only a matter of time.

"I took care of his needs and didn't complain. If he wanted anything, I made sure he got it," Ginny said. "I felt as if I had done everything expected. Where I failed—and this was the most important—was in my not considering his feelings, especially his fear."

Gramps didn't talk much about his fears, but Ginny sensed that fear was the biggest reason for his refusal to move. The nursing facility meant the final stage for him.

She couldn't correct her mistakes, but she constantly assured him of her love and made sure he got the best care possible.

"Each time I came, even if he was asleep, I read the Bible aloud to him," she said. "I chose mostly passages of encouragement. I wanted Gramps to hear words that would give him peace and remove his fear. You know something amazing? As Gramps has become more calm, so have I. Both of us are at peace now."

"I sought the LORD, and he answered me, and delivered me from all my fears" (Psalm 34:4).

Forgiving God, as I continue to ask you to give my loved one peace, grant me your peace. Remind me that you care and you're always with me—even when I make mistakes. Amen.

Those Daily Visits

"I thought taking care of my mother for four years was the hardest thing I'd ever have to do," Martha said. "But I found something worse—visiting her at the nursing facility."

Martha's story didn't seem that unusual, because I had heard it before. Some complaints had been even worse. "The odor is the first thing that hits your face when you walk inside," she said. "It's a kind of antiseptic smell, but it's still an odor."

I remembered my experiences as a pastor when I had to visit such places. One of them reeked with urine so strongly the first few times I backed out and gagged before I could go inside. Yes, I remembered well.

"People in wheelchairs lined the hallways with their hands stretched out," she said. "A few called out, but I couldn't understand what they were saying. Two or three of them tugged at my coat if I got too close." One woman in particular clutched her hand and held on. Martha had to fight to free herself.

"My mother is at the end of a hallway, and I have to pass several rooms. I see sad, wrinkled faces stare back at me. Some of them seem to have no idea who they are. I usually stare at my feet as I walk past those rooms."

For two months, Martha went to the skilled nursing facility every day, and it didn't get easier. "I wanted to run out of the place. When I got home, I showered after all those hands had pawed me."

A few times she's wished she could be sick and not have to go. Although Martha's mother is mentally alert, her severe physical problems need professional nursing.

"I love you, and I love being with you," Martha said to

her, "but it's so hard to come to this terrible place. I wish we could afford something better."

"Even if it were the best, would it make any difference?" her mother asked.

"Of course it would," Martha said. "For one thing, there wouldn't be all those people in wheelchairs in the hallway."

"In the afternoons after you leave, I have a nurse put me in my wheelchair. If I feel strong enough, I push myself down to the lounge," her mother said. "On the way, I talk to them. Even if I can't understand what they're saying, I smile, and they smile back."

Regretting that she had said anything, Martha tried to change the subject. She looked around the room and had to admit to herself that it was clean—small and a bit cramped, but definitely clean.

"You know why those people reach out and grab at you?" her mother asked. "They're lonely. They want someone to touch them, just to care about them. Some of them haven't had a visitor in months. The nurse told me."

"But they claw at me. I feel awful around them."

"They're just lonely, dear. Sad and lonely, that's all."

When Martha left, she avoided the others as much as she could. That night, however, she couldn't sleep. She'd close her eyes and think about those hands thrust at her. No matter how hard she tried to push them away, they kept coming at her. About dawn, she remembered a story Jesus told about separating sheep from goats—the good from the bad—at the end of the world. Jesus commended the sheep. Particularly, she remembered one thing Jesus said, "I was in prison and you visited me" (Matthew 25:36c).

Yes, Martha thought, those sad, lonely people are in a kind of prison. They're sentenced to remain and unable to leave. They'll probably die there. Tears filled her eyes when she thought how no one visits them.

Martha has changed since those days. It's still not easy for her to visit her mother, but now she looks at the other residents differently. She shakes hands. Occasionally, she hugs someone and pauses to speak to each one.

"Strange, but I think they're beginning to know me," she said.

Martha has learned a valuable lesson. Although she has a heavy load every day, she can still take a few minutes to reach out to others. She used to talk about her friends' being uncaring and insensitive. "Then I realized I wasn't much different. I wanted others to care for me and my mother, but I didn't want to bother with anyone else."

Martha is learning to extend her caring outreach. She says, "You know, it takes so little to be kind, doesn't it?"

[Jesus said] "Then the king will say to those at his right hand, 'Come, you that are blessed by my Father, inherit the kingdom prepared for you from the foundation of the world; . . . I was in prison and you visited me'" (Matthew 25:34, 36c).

God of compassion, I want people to reach out to me, but I've been reluctant to reach out to those who need my touch. Forgive me. Amen.

Telling the Truth

How much do we tell the loved one? Most of us would agree that we don't blurt out the harsh words that speak of a soon-approaching end. Most of us probably wouldn't go the other way and say, "Oh, you're going to be all right."

When my older brother Ray was dying of lung cancer, we talked about his life. He wanted me to tell him that he could beat the disease and that he'd be able to take his kids camping during the summer. I couldn't do that. The doctors had already alerted the family by saying, "Any day now."

I didn't want to discourage my brother, but I refused to give false assurance. That's the tricky line we sometimes have to walk.

Of course, the person we deal with makes the difference. I recall when the doctor told the family of an eighty-seven-year-old woman that their mother wouldn't leave the hospital alive, they didn't know what to say or do. She kept asking, "What did the doctor say?" They gave her vague answers.

Because I knew Annie well, I felt they were wrong not to tell her. She asked repeatedly, and I felt that indicated she did want to know. But even more, Annie was eighty-seven. "How do you think she got that old?" I asked the oldest daughter. "She's strong, perhaps stronger than you are. Tell her. Let her know the truth."

All five children went in at the same time and told her. She merely nodded and said, "I want them to sing 'What a Friend We Have in Jesus' at my funeral." She also wanted a soloist to sing "His Eye Is on the Sparrow." Then she surprised them by telling them where to find the list of phone numbers of far-off relatives to notify. "They're too old to come, but I want them to know."

In Annie's case, she could handle the information. She probably knew before the doctors did. Once the children were able to cope with that knowledge, she could express her last wishes. Annie died peacefully a few days later.

We're all different, and so are those we care for. I suggest that if the patient needs to be told and the caregiver can't do it, get someone who can. A pastor or a doctor or a close family friend can sometimes handle that. If the person doesn't really want to hear such news, he or she will let you know.

"How do you think you're doing?" is one question a nurse-friend sometimes asks. She gets the person talking—sometimes in whispers or short, labor-laden sentences. The responses guide her in how much to tell.

A third approach is what I call the oblique road. Some people can't speak plainly and don't want to hear direct answers. "When will I go home?" doesn't give much information, but it does indicate that the person doesn't expect to stay in the hospital.

"You'll leave the hospital in a few days," one woman said to her sister. "Then we're taking you to a nursing facility."

"Then will I go home?"

"No, dear."

Only two words, but they had the right impact. It was the way the sisters had communicated with each other during their lives together. They continued in the understated. For that family, it worked.

How much *do* we tell the loved one? My response is that we need to do a lot of soul searching and praying. I don't know the answer, but I do suggest to people, "Pray.

Ask for guidance. Keep praying until you feel right about a course of action. You'll know because you'll have inner peace about it."

When we follow that simple suggestion, it usually works. We get in tune with what's going on inside ourselves, and enables us to focus on the other person.

"We do not live to ourselves, and we do not die to ourselves. If we live, we live to the Lord, and if we die, we die to the Lord; so then, whether we live or whether we die, we are the Lord's" (Romans 14:7–8).

Guide me, O God, in how much to say and how much to hold back. Amen.

Just Saying No

"Are you going to take me home today?" she asks Andrea.

"Not today," she says. "Not today."

"I won't be any trouble. I promise I won't. I just want to go home to be with you and Ken."

"Mama, you can't come home right now. Maybe later." As soon as Andrea said "maybe later," she realized she had lied. Her mother wouldn't be coming home . A rush of guilt flooded through her for giving false hope.

For the rest of the visit, she kept thinking of what she had said. It would have been more honest to say, "No, Mama, you're not going home." A social worker had urged her to say no as succinctly as she could. Most of all, she wasn't to give her mother a reason.

"If you give her a reason, she'll keep trying to figure out ways to overcome that objection. A simple no has a finality about it."

Andrea knew the social worker was correct, but it was hard to say no to her mother. Every time Andrea visited the nursing facility—which was almost every day—her mother asked the same question.

Andrea began to realize that her problem in saying no went beyond the question of taking her mother home to live with her and her family again. It had always been hard. Whenever her mother wanted Andrea to do any-thing, she had always done it, even after she had her own family. Many times Andrea had wanted to refuse or to say she was busy when her mother wanted her immedi-ate help. Too often her mother had infringed on family time or made unreasonable demands. Andrea felt as if she was supposed to be there to take care of her mother's needs and forget her own.

As she pondered her evasive response, Andrea resolved that the next time she would answer honestly. She asked God for strength to speak the truth.

"Are you going to take me home today?" her mother asked the next day.

"No, mother. We will not be taking you home."

"You don't want me, is that it?"

"Mother, I won't be taking you home with us."

"Not ever?"

"No, not ever."

That settled it. Her mother never asked again. Later, Andrea wondered why she hadn't said those words before. She realized then that she couldn't have, because she hadn't resolved the dilemma herself. Until she was willing to say no to her mother about other things, she wasn't able to say no about going home.

Andrea still visits her mother almost every day. Her mother seems to have accepted life in her new surroundings. Outwardly, things remain much the same, but Andrea is different. Although she loves her mother, Andrea knows more than ever that she has a life apart from her.

"But speaking the truth in love, we must grow up in every way into him who is the head, into Christ" (Ephesians 4:15).

Strong and loving God, sometimes I find it difficult to speak the truth when the other doesn't want to hear it. Give me wisdom to speak the truth caringly. Amen.

The Future We Won't Have

My older brother Ray was dying of lung cancer at age fifty-three. About two months before he died, his wife, Katie, called me on the phone. "I just need to talk to someone," she said.

Katie was having a difficult time accepting the fact that she was going to lose her husband. They had married at age eighteen and had raised five children.

After she told me the diagnosis, she said, "I keep thinking about the future we won't have together." Katie wasn't an eloquent person, but she tried to explain the pain of a future life without Ray. He had been the only man in her life, and she couldn't think of how to live without him.

"He keeps talking about beating this, and of picking up the kids and grandkids and going camping," she said. "He talks about what he's going to do after he's licked this cancer."

Ray didn't beat the cancer. No matter how positively he spoke, Katie knew almost from the beginning how it would end. She didn't try to discourage him from dreaming and planning. But she knew.

When Ray spoke of things he wanted to do with the kids and how he wanted to add on to the house, Katie silently brooded on life without him.

"I always thought we'd grow old together," she said. "We would retire and maybe move out of the city. That's how Ray used to talk about our future." Several times she couldn't continue because of the tears and I waited for her to regain control.

"There isn't any future for us, is there? We're never going to do those things."

As she talked, I remembered the old-fashioned pressure cooker my mother used during my growing-up years. The food cooked away on the stove as the pressure built up in the cooker, which was tightly sealed with a lid. When the pressure reached a certain point, my mother would release the valve, and let the steam out.

That's how I heard Katie's call. The pressure had built up. Her husband was dying. To focus on the future they wouldn't have together was her way of looking reality in the face. She was entering a new phase in her life, and she needed to explore it, to feel it, to talk about it.

Looking back, I remember the long pauses when she cried. Tears weren't something I had ever associated with Katie. At one point, I thought she would have to hang up because the hurt overwhelmed her so.

For Katie, crying was probably the best thing she could do for herself. Facing the future meant half a life and emptiness. Of course, she eventually adjusted after Ray's death. But that came later. That night she was caught in her inner turmoil.

I'm glad she called me. Caregivers need those people who will listen without trying to solve their problems or lay out the solutions. In reality, no matter what I said, it wouldn't have made much difference. Katie had to work through the dilemma herself because it was her battle.

After she hung up, I thought of the spiritual "Lonesome Valley." It says we have to go there by ourselves, and nobody else can do it for us. No one else can take away our pain because it's *our* pain.

Maybe the best we can hope for is that as we walk through that lonesome valley God is always with us, and that a few caring people will embrace us. Perhaps one or two will whisper, "I love you even when you're hurting."

"For he has said, 'I will never leave you or forsake you.' So we can say with confidence, 'The Lord is my helper; I will not be afraid'" (Hebrews 13:5b–6a).

God of eternity, you are my future and the only certainty I have in this life. Thank you for being with me always. Even when the future seems bleak, you are with me. Amen.

When Will This Be Over?

"Will this never end? Am I going out of my mind? I'm scared I'm going to lose her, and yet I wish she would just go ahead and die."

Any of those words may come to long-term care-givers. The ambiguity of the situation may feel so engulf-ing that caregivers feel they can no longer cope. And for that moment, they can't. The inescapable nature of con-stant care causes them to feel angry and resentful, and they may even say or pray things they wish they could take back.

"I hadn't meant to say that I wished he'd die," Grace said. "But I said it—out loud and to myself. Deep remorse struck as soon as the words came out. Yet they're true. At least part of the time, I do want Dad to die. I'm tired, and I want to get out from under all this pressure. My husband and my two kids pull at me from one direc-tion and my dying father from the other."

The words slipped out of Grace's mouth. They had been deep within her heart for a long time, but she had never allowed herself to think consciously of her dad's dying. Especially, that she would *want* him to die.

"Most of us feel that way when we're tired, or had a bad day, or the person gets too demanding," Marlene said.

"I know, but it seems so—so heartless and mean."

"Would it be easier to say, 'I wish God would take him out of his misery'?" Marlene asked. She went on to say, "It's really only a matter of framing your words. It's okay to feel. You can't control your emotions."

For a long time Grace didn't say anything. I had asked both women to talk to me about just this topic. Unable to look directly at us, Grace said haltingly, "I love my

232

father, and I don't know what life would be like without him."

"But you don't want him to suffer any more?" Marlene asked helpfully. "Surely you think, he's suffered enough."

Grace agreed and added, "I know it's only a matter of time. Yet it seemed wrong, almost sinful, to ask God to take him."

"Someone in my support group said, 'You can't choose your feelings, but you can choose your actions.' That helped tremendously," Marlene said. "When I chose to keep my mother, I decided to be there as long as she needed me. Yet my feelings fluctuate. Sometimes, I want it to end and cry out to God to lift the burden."

"And both of us know that when it is over," Grace said, "we'll experience pain, loss, and emptiness, won't we?"

Others have told me the same thing. Those feelings of wanting the ordeal to end may come as fleeting thoughts or may even be constantly present.

Marlene again helped by expressing her vulnerability, "When I think of my mother dying because it would end her suffering, I know that's a good kind of desire. My guilt arises when I want her gone to make it easier for me."

The following week I spoke to Grace again. "All my friends who care for loved ones tell me it's a normal reaction and the same thing," she said, "but it's a terrible jolt, and I think I must be a terrible person. Now, I realize I'm just being human."

Long-term caring drains us emotionally, spiritually, physically, and financially. When there's no other possible outcome, it's natural to want the struggle to end—for everybody's sake. When we admit to such feelings, we're also recognizing that we're less than perfect. We're being true to who we really are.

"Even before a word is on my tongue, O LORD, you know it completely. . . . Search me, O God, and know my heart; test me and know my thoughts" (Psalm 139:4, 23).

God of all knowledge, thank you for understanding not only the words I pray but also the emotions behind them. Amen.

Emotional Regulation

Wendy has expressed concern for weeks about her mother. "She used to be so vital, so interested in life. She liked learning new things and meeting people. Now she's withdrawn from almost everything."

"Does she refuse to see anyone?" a member of Wendy's support group asked.

"She sees family members and old friends, but I can't interest her in investigating activities or meeting new people."

Wendy planned a dinner party for her mother's birthday. She was going to take her from the nursing facility for an overnight visit. She had already reserved a room at what had been her mother's favorite restaurant, and invited everyone in their two-hundred-member church to come. Before her mother became ill, this would have been an exciting event for her.

"I don't want to go," her mother said when she first heard about the event.

"But Mama, you like these things. You'll meet a lot of nice people."

"I don't want to meet any people. I'm going to die soon anyway."

Two members of the support group understood. They were caregivers of people with similar attitudes. "You're focusing on the future," one woman said. "That's not what your mother thinks about. She's living in the present. She's focusing on the now."

As they talked, Wendy began to realize that she needed to offer her mother things that were present oriented and that brought her immediate pleasure.

"She's not interested in long-term payoff, such as meeting new people," the other woman said. "Why should she invest her time and energy in something that might pay off in a friendship in a year? She's not interested in learning about computers or speaking French."

Emotional regulation is the term for this. Caregivers can do such things as plan parties if they approach the event as something to enjoy *today*. "Your friends want to see you." Or, "I just thought you'd feel better being around a few people today and enjoy talking with others." As their life shrinks, so does their world. Rather than seeing this as depression or giving up, it's helpful if caregivers can accept this as a natural shift in the person's progress.

It took Wendy a few days to absorb that fact. When she returned to the support group, she beamed. "Yes, yes, I understand. That is God's way of preparing her to leave us. If she still wanted to do things and go places, it would show she's nowhere near ready. As she slowly cuts off the outside interests, she becomes more focused internally."

Wendy's last months with her mother turned out to be the best in the five years of illness. "I kept tuned into the present. If she wanted to talk about the past, as she often did, that was fine. She wanted to see a few old friends, but she had no interest in whether the Braves won the pennant or whether it would rain. It was a gradual, almost subtle, moving forward."

Wendy accepted this as her mother's internal preparation. Rather than trying to hinder or divert her, she supported the shift in attitude. "I think it helped make Mama's last days more comfortable," she said.

"God is our refuge and strength, a very present help in trouble" (Psalm 46:1).

God of time and eternity, when my loved one turns inward and shuts out the world, help me focus on you and know that you're very close to both of us. Amen.

Talking about Death

"Do we have to talk about it now?" Rich's mother asked. "It—it sounds so gloomy."

That day they didn't talk about her funeral, a will, what to do about her house, or any of her final wishes. They didn't talk about them the next day either—or the next month. Rich's mother died before he ever learned what kind of funeral she wanted, and she didn't leave a will.

"I wish I had persisted," Rich said. "If only we could have talked just once, but she'd never do that."

As Rich learned, dealing with an aging parent can be difficult. Some people face the end more openly and realistically than others. We know that sooner or later death comes to us all. Too many treat it as the unspoken taboo. We can talk about death in general or about the loss of a friend or neighbor, but it's difficult to face our own demise.

Rich now speaks of the anger he feels because he and his mother never discussed final matters. He has gone through a lot of legal entanglements with his mother's investments. "I try not to feel anger, but I do," he said. "She could have made it so simple."

Not facing the inevitable can not only cause problems after death, but can also exacerbate problems in the present. Harsh words slip out; unkind remarks get made. Sometimes we hold in mixed feelings and can't concentrate on giving our parents the best and most loving thoughts.

Myron handled this area well. Years ago he heard a lecture in which the person said something to the effect that, "If we fail to work through our mixed feelings for a parent who depends on us, we may undermine our own health and badly affect family relationships."

"I never forgot those words," he said, even though it would be years before he had to face them. He did have mixed feelings toward his mother. He loved her, but she had hurt him in many ways.

Myron believed that by not pushing his mother to look ahead realistically, he was making it much more difficult for her to face what lay ahead.

"Mom, we need to talk about your future," he said after her first heart attack.

"Oh, don't be so morbid," his mother said. "It depresses me. We need to think positively right now."

"It's not morbidity; it's reality. I'm all for positive thinking, so why don't you think positively about the future. I don't think you're going to leave us soon, but I want us to be ready when you do go. Don't you want the details taken care of? If we do that, then we can concentrate on caring for you."

With some reluctance, his mother consented. Afterward she said, "It's a relief, really. It's done, and now I don't have to think about it anymore."

Sometimes it goes the other way. Many times the parents have tried to talk to their offspring about dying, but the adult children can't handle it. "You're going to be fine," they say. "There's plenty of time for that. Do we have to talk about it now?"

A wise parent insists, "Yes, for *my* peace of mind."

Regardless of who starts it or who insists, the discussion needs to be done. It clears the air. It brings the reality of life and death into the open. It's a way of acknowledging to all parties that "Mom won't live forever."

In our culture, we tend to deny the reality—and the finality—of death. Yet it comes to each of us. The more openly we can face it, the easier on everyone concerned, especially after death takes place.

When I think about the honest handling of this, I think of two people who handled it straightforwardly. First, Edith. Within a year after her health began to fail, she brought up the legal issues. She insisted that Shirley have a medical power of attorney and changed her checking account so that both could sign checks. She updated her will. She contacted the firm that handled her investments. Although they were not large, she arranged that Shirley or she could make withdrawals or payments. That investment money paid for most of the months she spent in the skilled nursing home, and Shirley drew out funds as needed.

There were other considerations such as burial or cremation. Edith chose a burial society and cremation, so that heavy load was taken from us.

Ann Samples handled my taxes for years and was a member of the Riverdale Presbyterian Church during my ten years as pastor. Long ago, before she became sick with leukemia, she said, "Wherever you are, when I die, I want you to conduct my funeral."

Ann died in late 1999. A few weeks before her death, she called me from her hospital bed. "You know it won't be long now," she said. "I want to remind you that I want you to take care of my funeral."

Both Edith and Ann faced the end with courage far beyond that of most people. They knew that to talk about death with those we care for isn't easy. Often it means tears and pain. But the pain is temporary. "It's preparation," Edith said, "and it will make things easier for you when I do go." She was right, of course.

Death can be a fearful thing. I've always believed that if we face our fear, we can conquer it. We conquer by talking and by taking necessary steps to prepare our loved one for it. Isn't it an act of kindness to take away the fear—to remove it from both the caregiver and the one cared for?

A final word: If you can't talk about death—if you find it impossible to discuss it—accept that as your limitation. Ask someone who can, such as a pastor or a health-care professional. What seems the most frightening, when faced, can be the most liberating.

"The time of my departure has come. I have fought the good fight, I have finished the race, I have kept the faith. From now on there is reserved for me the crown of righteousness, which the Lord, the righteous judge, will give me on that day" (2 Timothy 4:6b–8a).

Immortal God, death frightens me. I can't imagine life without my being part of it. My loved one surely feels the same way. Help us to face it courageously, knowing that even in death we are in your loving hands. Amen.

Preparing for the End

"I can't do it," Shirley said. "I just can't."

Because I sensed the struggle my wife was going through, I hugged her and held her. "It's for you to decide."

Edith had deteriorated to the point where she was demanding almost around-the-clock care. She lived in a mother-in-law suite downstairs in our home, and that meant going up and down an extra flight of stairs throughout the day. Shirley had her own health problems, but she didn't complain. She spent increasing amounts of time with Edith.

As I watched the situation, I realized that all of us have a breaking point—the time when we say, "I can't do it any longer." Obviously, some reach that place before others. Shirley had held up for nearly six years.

Then came a time for us to evaluate and decide. The surgeon wanted to operate for colon cancer. Edith could then go directly to the nursing facility. If she came home first, we would have to put her on a waiting list when we were ready for her to go. That often took months.

"I'll let you know. I need to think and pray about it," Shirley told the doctor. At home, she said to me, "If I send her there, I'll feel as if I've failed."

I felt it was the right time for Edith to go to the nursing facility, but because Shirley was the primary caregiver, it had to be her decision. I expressed my opinion, but I assured her I was agreeable to whatever she did.

When Edith's only brother, who has severe heart problems and lives in another state, visited us and saw the gravity of the situation, he agreed with the surgeon. "Edith will accept it, and she won't feel you're failing her. You just can't bring her back here after the surgery, even if the physician thinks he was able to get all the cancer."

Shirley still hesitated.

The most significant argument came from Edith's pastor, Dave Siefried, who regularly visited. One day after he had been with Edith, he came upstairs to visit Shirley.

"If you don't send her," he said, "she will become your life. Because of her condition, she'll need more care than you can give her. She'll need someone during the night and all through the day. You'll never have time for your husband, your children, your own church, or your friends. Edith will be your life—your total life."

Dave's visit persuaded Shirley. Reluctantly, she made arrangements.

For several days after Edith's transfer from the hospital, Shirley suffered from guilt and feelings of failure. Every day when she came home after visiting Edith, she would say, "I should be able to take care of her." As Edith's condition deteriorated, Shirley said the words less often. The day came when she said, "Pastor Dave was right. Unless I totally devoted my life to her, I couldn't do it."

It had been a difficult decision for Shirley. When I've spoken with other longer-term caregivers, they've said the same thing. Who could feel good about such a decision? Some might feel relieved that the burden was lifted, but deep within, guilt would still lurk.

"A voice kept whispering, 'You could have done it a little longer,'" one caregiver said.

"For the first time in five years, I was able to sleep through an entire night without getting up," said a friend before tears filled her eyes. "It just didn't seem right."

Difficult or easy, caregivers eventually must make

such decisions. It is, for them and for the one they love, preparation for the end. Shirley now looks back and says, "I didn't want to let go, but it was the right decision."

Even the right decision can be painful. And many caregivers realize their need to rely on the One who understands and strengthens them to do what needs doing.

"I can do all things through him who strengthens me" (Philippians 4:13).

God of comfort and compassion, perhaps there is no easy way for me to surrender those I love. Thank you for guiding and strengthening me in that decision. Amen.

"Why Doesn't God Take Me?"

"Why doesn't God take me?" Janet's husband asked. "I'm no good to anyone like this. I'm just taking up space on this earth and causing you a lot of work and problems."

It wasn't the first time he had asked the question. He was suffering from Lou Gehrig's disease and growing increasingly incapacitated. He had been a top college athlete, always a vigorous, robust man. He had entered the business world by taking over an almost-defunct real estate office just outside a metropolitan city. Through advertising and attracting builders to reshape the community, Matt had become one of the brightest lights in the business.

Matt and Janet had raised two healthy children, both now married with children of their own. Everything was going right for Matt, until increasing physical weakness halted his career. From then on, he grew weaker and more despondent.

"Help me end this suffering," he begged.

Janet knew what he meant, but she couldn't do such a thing.

"I'm just no good to you or to anybody," Matt said.

Despite his success in business and the affection of his family, Matt saw no use in living.

Matt went slowly downhill, as he and Janet knew he would. Lou Gehrig's disease is a disease that's been fairly well studied for the past half century, although there is no known cure. "All I know is that God wants you here," she would say.

Only near the end of his life did Matt slowly begin to grasp an important fact—something that eluded him all his life. As his body weakened, Matt began to reflect on life, asking why God kept him alive. "You know, I am of value to God," he said one morning. "I don't understand that or know why, but just by being alive—a creation of God—that gives me value, doesn't it?"

Janet agreed. The tears were too close to the surface to speak, so she squeezed his hand.

"I always thought that I had to accomplish, to prove myself, to be productive and that gave me value." He slowly shook his head, one of the few gestures he could still make. "I got it all wrong. All these years, and I've had it wrong."

Matt and Janet talked more intimately over the next month than they ever had. As Matt's days drew closer to the end, he began to appreciate life. "I don't have to do anything for God to love me, do I?"

At age fifty-eight, Matt realized that no matter how hard he worked, he could never do anything to make God love him more. "And there's nothing I could do that would make God love me less, is there?"

Each day as Matt moved toward his last breath, he and Janet asked for what he termed "dying grace." One time he prayed, "God, help me live each moment in this life as long as you're willing to leave me here. Let me also be ready when the final moment comes."

Matt stopped asking to die; he didn't plead to live either. He learned to accept life as it came and to enjoy each day.

The biggest pleasure they shared together was to watch the sunset from their hilltop home. "God puts on a great show for me every night," Matt said.

Afterward, Janet said, "By the way Matt died, he taught me the joy of living and being thankful for each day."

Like many long-term caregivers, it was an important lesson for her to learn and to cherish.

"Who will separate us from the love of Christ? Will hardship, or distress, or persecution, or famine, or nakedness, or peril, or sword? . . . No, in all these things we are more than conquerors through him who loved us" (Romans 8:35, 37).

God of light and truth, it's hard to understand life and your ways. Make me teachable. Amen.

Lessons from the Dying

"Give, give, give, that's all I did for nine years," one disgruntled woman said. "I loved my husband, but it's finally over and now I can take care of myself."

I sat with a group of five women at a senior citizen's center in an Atlanta suburb and asked them to share their experiences in long-term caregiving. Three of the women echoed the first woman's words and quickly added their own story.

The most significant response came from Ann, who was the last to speak. "There's one thing none of you have mentioned," she said. "You've talked about giving yourselves. You've talked about the loneliness, the hurtful neglect of others." She reflected on some of their comments. "But none of you have talked about receiving. We can learn many things from the dying, you know."

That was the first quiet moment in the group. Each seemed to pull back into a private space and reflect on what Ann had said. She had married a man who suffered through periods of deep depression. One day he shot himself twice in the abdomen. He survived, but for the next fourteen years he was able to do little more than move the upper part of his body.

"I learned so much from Aubrey," Ann said. "I learned to listen. I hadn't been good at that before, because I had to be on the go, always rushing about with the kids and doing the things I felt I had to do. But day after day I learned to sit beside Aubrey and hold his hand. He began to talk."

She said that she had learned more about him in those fourteen years than she had known in the thirty-one that went before them. "Before, I had no idea how strongly he felt or how much he hurt inside." Ann talked about his dimples and quick smile and acerbic wit that made everyone think he was always fine. "But he wasn't, and I didn't know that. Not really. His episodes of depression, well, I thought they were passing things, little interludes. It was really the other way around."

In various ways, the other four women said they had learned some of the same things. Their dying husbands had enabled them to look inward and to think differently about life. As I've continued to speak with caregivers, I sometimes asked, "Tell me a few of the lessons you've learned from the dying."

Carole Fulmer, not one of the group, e-mailed me a list of ten things she had learned. Here are a few of them: "A greater closeness, because I dropped everything other than doing for others, and devoted myself to my husband; a satisfaction of doing something for someone who had great needs and was little understood; satisfaction from helping him to function at his highest level; patience in big doses. Some of my friends thought I was too patient because I allowed him to take as long as he wanted to eat when we went to a restaurant. I allowed him to fix his plate even when I could have prepared it faster. He was my focus."

When I read the list to the women, they nodded.

"Yes, I agree, and we need reminding of that too, don't we? It's easy to forget that life is more than giving," said the woman who had started out complaining so vocally.

"Too often we think we're the only ones who have anything to give," said another. "But we do receive, often in amazing, intangible ways."

"Teach me your way, O LORD, that I may walk in your truth; give me an undivided heart to revere your name" (Psalm 86:11).

God of wisdom, teach me whatever I need to know, and let me learn from those I'm caring for. Amen.

Empty Spaces

"Oh, for a minute, I thought—" Shirley's mother put her hand over her mouth, slightly embarrassed. "Your shoe—it look liked my husband's. He wore black ones like that, and his were about the same size. He'd sometimes take them off when he was relaxing."

Shirley's father had been dead four years before we started to date. I had come to her house that evening to get acquainted with her mother. In a relaxed mood, I had kicked off my shoes. Because Shirley's mother had been caught off guard, the shoe brought back memories of her late husband.

A moment like that is really not that unusual.

Others tell about little things, events that trigger memories. "Every once in a while something momentarily fills the empty spaces the loved one used to be in," one woman said. "It's fleeting, but it happens."

One man spoke of loving to watch his wife's hands as she knitted—something she did most nights when they watched the TV news. One woman said that for months, whenever she went past Baskin & Robbins, she wanted to turn to her husband and ask, "Do you want some ice cream?"

Empty spaces, those objects or events of memory, are the places we associate with a loved one. Some of them are so ingrained that it's hard to separate a place from the loved one.

"I worked late," Dorothy Baker said, "and my husband worried about me. When I pulled into the driveway, I'd see him sitting by the window, watching for me. As soon as I made the turn in, he'd flip on the outside light. I still work late, but the lights never go on," she said. "Yet I'm amazed at how often I expect it to happen."

One woman told me that her husband loved gospel quartet music. Sometimes, she'll sit in a darkened room, turn on the stereo, and play one of his favorite CDs. She has never been a big fan of that kind of music. "It may sound strange, but it helps me feel his presence. As I sit in the unlit room, I can almost see him tapping his left foot in time to the music."

Those are difficult memories. And sometimes tears flow, even when the person is still alive. It's a place we associate with one we love.

Unfortunately, too many think they need to push away such empty spaces. "If you're going to get over this," a well-intentioned friend says, "you have to stop thinking that way."

I don't agree. If our hand touches our loved one's favorite chair and we think of his sitting there reading, we don't have to berate ourselves for still missing him.

In fact, maybe it works better if we change our thinking about such empty places. Maybe it's not only healthy to keep memories alive; perhaps it is also comforting to us.

My friend Margie Hunter said that for months after he died, she kept her husband's room exactly as it had been. "I needed to go in there and feel his presence, to think of the years we spent together. Memories were all I had left of our thirty-nine years together."

Despite our anxiety to help people get over their grief and fill the empty spaces, I think of the many memorial events we find in the Old Testament. Jacob had a dream at Bethel and set up a stone to memorialize it. Under Joshua's leadership, the people crossed the Jordan River on dry land. Before the water returned, Joshua ordered the people to put twelve stones in the river as a memorial of the event.

Such gestures still happen today, and I think they are helpful. For perhaps a month, I used to see a white cross with flowers just off the shoulder along I-85 north of Atlanta. A young woman had died in a car crash, and I assume that her family memorialized her that way. The Department of Transportation people eventually took it down, but until they did, I like to think the family found consolation whenever they saw the cross.

Why those empty spaces? I'm not sure, but I suspect that something of our loved ones remain. It may be only a flash of thought, a lingering movement, but something fills in the empty space. And we need something concrete to fasten our eyes on. For some, stained-glass windows do it—or a burial plot. The object itself doesn't seem as important as the memories it triggers.

When I was a boy, my mother used a particular kind of face powder. I never knew the brand, but I've never forgotten how it smelled. Whenever the fragrance touches my nostrils, I'm momentarily thrown into that empty space. I can see her in front of a mirror dusting her face.

Is it possible that God brings these empty spaces into our lives? Is it not conceivable that they may come to aid us, to help us release those we love? I wonder if the first followers of Jesus felt that way when they observed what we call the Lord's Supper or the Eucharist. To the Corinthian Church, Paul wrote about the proper observance of that event. He quoted Jesus as saying of the bread, "This is my body that is for you. Do this in remembrance of me" (1 Corinthians 11:24b). He gave them the cup and concluded with "Do this, as often as you drink it, in remembrance of me" (25b).

Perhaps the empty spaces—which aren't really empty after all—have a place in our lives. When our loved ones are in the hospital or in a nursing home, or even after they're gone, those empty spaces are there for our comfort. They are there to help us remember—not to forget.

[Jesus said] "And remember, I am with you always, to the end of the age" (Matthew 28:20b).

God of all memory, help me remember those I love. As long as I need to fill in the empty spaces, enable me to do that with joy. Enable me to realize that my loved one fills that space in my heart. Amen.